D1649010

HEART
of a
MULE

DICK SCHAFRATH

HEART of a MULE

GRAY & COMPANY, PUBLISHERS
CLEVELAND

Gray & Company, Publishers
www.grayco.com

ISBN 1-59851-024-X

Printed in the United States of America

10 9 8 7 6 5 4 3 2 1

CONTENTS

FOREWORD

BY JIM BROWN
NFL Hall of Fame

Senator Dick Schafrath—my friend, my teammate—is one of the most extraordinary human beings I have ever met. As a teammate, he displayed impeccable work ethics. He drove himself tirelessly to excellence. Probably the greatest overachiever I ever met. Always pushing himself mentally and physically.

During the 1960s, the Cleveland Browns had one of the best offensive lines of all time. Never getting the credit they deserved, Dick Schafrath and Gene Hickerson were two all-stars of that time. Their attention to detail, their strength at point of attack, their speed downfield resulted in a 5.2 average per carry for yours truly, number 32.

I always marveled at Dick's tenacity. He never showed fatigue, never considered giving up or giving in. On some plays he would actually get three blocks. If a player was opposite him, Schaf took care of business first, then sprinted downfield to try to make another block. Finally, with speed and determination, he would get in front of me to try to block the last defender. Dick and Gene definitely gave us the greatest line in the history of Cleveland football.

I could go on and on, but the greatest compliment I can give Dick is that he should be in the Hall of Fame. It seems strange that he and Gene Hickerson, the heart of the line that produced three Hall of Fame runners, are not in the Hall themselves.

Football is just one source of my admiration for the Mule. His friendship has always been consistent. Being a conservative with no personal or racial bias might seem a strange combination to most people in the world. But that's Dick.

The Amer-I-Can program, which teaches life skills to young adults, is in twenty-two schools in the state of Ohio and has proven itself to be an effective program. The only way it was possible was through the efforts of Senator Dick Schafrath, who worked tirelessly each year to make sure the program was funded.

If anyone ever needed a favor, or if a team ever needed an assistant coach at any level, you would see the Mule being the first to volunteer for the challenge. He canoed seventy-nine miles across Lake Erie, wrestled a bear at trade shows, and ran sixty-two miles nonstop. I wouldn't be surprised to learn that he climbed a mountain with nothing but his hands. He's crazy enough to try anything once.

This is a man I affectionately call my friend. Senator Dick Schafrath, "the Mule," "Schaf," a great teammate, a great American, and a great human being.

FOREWORD

BY JIM TRESSEL

Head Football Coach, The Ohio State University

A difference-maker. That is the best description I could possibly give of the Mule, Dick Schafrath. Wherever he is, whoever he is with, his goal is to make a positive difference. Every person and every situation improves when Dick Schafrath is near. He has made such a difference in so many lives and as a part of countless groups!

Anyone who has had the good fortune to know the Mule would agree that he was and is a fierce competitor. Whether a high school, collegiate, or professional athlete, or a member of the state senate, he was going to excel and win for the good of the team/group. Many fine folks have looked across the line at Dick and could see in his eyes that they were in for a battle royale!

If one asked Dick Schafrath what his most important roles have been, he would respond that he is, first, a humble child of God; second, a servant to others; third, a friend to many; and fourth, a very fortunate father.

Each week the Mule writes a message to our Ohio State Football family in which he challenges all of us to excel—first as men of God, and second as warriors on the gridiron. He has motivated so many Buckeyes as we strive to be the "difference-makers" ourselves that he has been for Wooster, Ohio; The Ohio State University; the Cleveland Browns; the state of Ohio; and all of his friends and wonderful family!

It has been an honor to be counted among the multitudes that have gained from knowing Dick Schafrath.

GROWING UP

CHAPTER ONE

HOMESPUN FARM LIVING

SALT OF THE EARTH

My story starts with my parents.

Each was the oldest of eleven children. Together they had seven children. When they died, they had twenty-nine grandchildren and fifteen great-grandchildren.

I am the oldest of five boys and two girls. One girl was stillborn. Our parents were Catholic and wanted each of us to be a priest or a nun. My brother Ed came closest. He had seven years of preparation in a seminary, but just before he was to be ordained he took a leave of absence. Now he has six children, so I don't think he will make it either.

Late one afternoon when my parents were nearly eighty years old, I stopped by to visit them. Mom was in the living room. Her elbows and knees were skinned and bleeding. Her hair was messy, her dress was torn, she had cuts on her face, and she had lost her glasses and one of her shoes. Before I could ask her what happened, Dad came limping into the living room from the opposite door.

He also had cuts and bruises. His glasses were bent and broken. His hat was muddy and twisted sideways. He was covered from head to toe with stinking cow manure. I was stunned, but before I could find out what happened, they both laughed at the looks of each other and came together for a big hug. That's the way I will always picture them. Truly, the salt of the earth.

It seems that Mom had gone to the mailbox at the end of the driveway when a speeding car came down the road and scared her. She fell into the ditch on her back. It took her nearly a half hour to roll over, crawl out, get back on her feet, and make the hundred yards to the house. She left her glasses and one shoe in the ditch.

Meanwhile, Dad had been in the barnyard putting hay in the cow racks. His pesky young bull had caught him off guard, knocked him down, and was rolling him around in the manure. Dad somehow got hold of his five-foot-long two-by-four, whacked him on the nose, and, as Dad said, "I ran, jumped over the fence like a rabbit and escaped."

Both were quite lucky. They immediately started caring for each other by cleaning their wounds. They never thought of going to a doctor or calling an insurance company. It was just another normal day at the farm. They were simple, humble, hard-working farm folks who dedicated their lives to helping family, neighbors, and friends. They never missed a Sunday at church or an evening saying the rosary. Doors were never locked—no visitor was a stranger. They never traveled very far from home. To them, Ohio was the United States and Wooster was the capital.

DAD

Dad was born in 1909 in Canton, Ohio, of German lineage (Rohr-Schafrath). As the oldest child, Dad was raised to support his family. He finished school after eighth grade, worked daily at two full-time jobs, and helped on the dairy farm during his spare time. He turned his paychecks over to his parents until he was twenty-one. His family moved to a farm on the east side of Wooster when he was sixteen. His father loved music, mainly accordion and piano, and played most every Saturday night with a local square dance band. Dad liked listening to music and loved to dance. He learned to call square dances with his father's band. He also learned of a tradition that if you had an ear of colored Indian corn in your hands, you could kiss the first girl you saw. He always carried an ear of Indian corn in his hip pocket and was ready whenever the occasion presented itself. Mom once told me that back when she was single, a man would always tell the girl he wanted to drive home to save the last dance for him. Dad always made sure he asked her, but one time he forgot. He never had to be reminded again. In fact, Dad was so upset he asked her to marry him. She said yes.

Dad lived to work. His work ethic reminds me of an old proverb: Every morning in Africa, a gazelle wakes up. It knows it must run faster than the fastest lion or it will be killed. Every morning a lion wakes up. It knows it must outrun the slowest gazelle or it will starve to death. It doesn't matter whether you are a lion or a gazelle—when the sun comes up, you'd better be running!

Dad never had the opportunity or the time to play sports. To him, they were a waste of time and effort. His game was work. He'd work night and day if people had something for him to do. He was strong as an ox and had great endurance. No one could ever outlast him. Whether it was cutting wood, loading hay, shocking wheat, milking cows, husking corn, planting, plowing, or mowing, he was like a machine. Back when I was a little guy, maybe five or six years old, I'd accompany Dad to the woods, where we'd cut down a tree for firewood with a big, two-man, 8-foot crosscut saw. Dad would say, "Okay, Dick, grab the other end of this ol' thing and let's start making sparks." It was one of those push-and-pull types—all MANpower. No matter the size of the tree, we'd start cutting, and he'd never stop until the tree came down. Sometimes I pushed on the saw, sometimes I pulled on the saw, sometimes I just hung on and watched. Sometimes I stopped and rested, but that saw never stopped cutting.

I do have fond memories of him resting occasionally. I don't think anyone else ever witnessed that. When I was real young, Dad and I sometimes would work at neighbors' farms. We traveled with our horses or mules pulling our wagon. Sometimes we'd take two wagons; then it was always a race to see who would get there first. At the end of the day, when we were on our way home, Dad would sometimes lie back on some loose hay and say, "How about a little relaxing?" We'd lie together and watch the sky with the trees and telephone wires going by. The dirt road was seldom traveled. The mules would always go straight for home. They knew where their food and bed was.

A strict Catholic, Dad never ate meat on Fridays, rarely missed church on Sundays, and led the family in saying the rosary every night. Before every meal, Dad always said the same prayer: "Oh

Lord, bless the gifts of thy bounty of which we are about to partake . . . in Jesus' name. Amen." One time he asked me to say the prayer. I wanted to be a smart-aleck, so I said something like, "Name of the Father, Son, and Holy Ghost, the one who eats the fastest gets the most." WHAM! I thought my head had come off my shoulders.

Every night immediately after our farm chores were finished, it was hair-cutting time. The dining room would start filling up with people. Euchre cards were dealt. (Dad was a great euchre player. In fact, the local Knights of Columbus sent him to Cleveland to play in an interstate tournament, and he won the top trophy.) Ice-cold water and cider were filled to the brim in pitchers. Hot buttered popcorn started popping and storytelling began. Dad was at center stage cutting hair. He never went to barber school, but nobody cared. The haircuts took two to five minutes. A nickel, dime, or quarter would go into the tithing bucket. I borrowed a lot of change from the bucket and plan to give it back someday. Dads from all around the county would come and bring their sons. It was a great bargain! Haircuts, card playing, storytelling, all the popcorn they could eat and all the (hard or sweet) cider they could drink. Mom usually had to push people out the door after 10 p.m. so we could say the rosary and go to sleep.

Dad loved animals and they loved him. Sometimes he'd drive them to market to sell. Sometimes he'd get sad and bring them back home. But he wasn't soft if it was work. He expected you to work as hard as he did. He seldom said much. He'd nod or smile his approval, and he frowned or whacked you if he disapproved.

Until the mid-1950s, when he was in his forties, Dad did all of his farming like the Amish—by hand, horses, and mules. If there was wheat to be shocked, he wanted to shock alone or with me. A shock would consist of standing eight or ten sheaves in a round stack, grains up, with one sheaf sprawled over the top to cover all the others. He could shock eight to ten acres in a day. Normally, it would take four, five, or six people to do that.

Dad's means of travel was walking, the horse and buggy, a Model-T Ford, and finally, a beat-up old Chevrolet pickup truck (if going to town). He treated rich and poor people the same. He never lied, was loyal, trustworthy, and dependable. If you paid him a penny too much, he'd drive fifty miles to return it. A tough disciplinarian, he expected you to know what you had to do without being told. When he did tell you something, he depended on you to follow through until the job was done.

One of the lasting memories I have of Dad was the formal use, discipline, and trust of a handshake. He said it was your seal of approval for everything. Once you shook hands and looked the person in the eye, it meant *I trust you and you can trust me.* Most farm deals were confirmed with a handshake. Need help? I'll be there when you start. Need to borrow equipment or use something? Just put it back where you got it when finished. Even to date a girl you had to meet and shake hands with her father for approval and trust. That tradition went out the window a long time ago.

A FEW OF DAD'S PET SAYINGS

When you discover the horse you're riding is dead, dismount! It won't go any farther.

No one ever died from their own sweat.

A person will not respect anything unless they earn it.

When work's done we can quit.

Don't let the cows run the ranch.

Half of doing the job is getting started. The other half is don't quit until the job is done.

There are no guarantees in life. You must re-earn your pay every day.

At nine o'clock at night: Okay boys, you can have the rest of the day off.

MOM

Mom was of Dutch-Irish descent (Starr-Lynch). Born in 1911, she grew up in the same brick house we were raised in. She had five brothers and five sisters. She was the oldest.

When Mom was young, she attended a one-room schoolhouse

about a mile from home. She walked to school with all her brothers and sisters. She always told them what to do—a trait that earned her the lifelong nicknames "Gabby" and "Boss." Mom was a good student and helped the teacher teach the other kids in all subjects. Her teacher, Don Welsh, taught me and, years later, one of my kids! He once told me that Mom was picked as captain of all of the school's sport teams and was selected as the outstanding athlete every year in grades four through eight. She went on to Wooster High School and graduated. She was definitely about team.

Mom had a job at the Wooster Pickle Works for a few years. Besides helping on the farm, Dad worked at Wooster Products, where they made iron pipe, and at Gertzenslager's, where they made postal trucks.

Dad would always stop over at the Pickle Works and help Mom sort the good pickles from the bad pickles and count the barrels. As strong as an ox, he would also throw the pickle barrels on the trucks so she could finish early. In fact, each week he'd pick up two huge blocks of ice—nearly two hundred pounds each!—all by himself. He'd load them onto the truck using ice clamps, then unload them into our springhouse shed to keep milk and other things cold.

Mom was allergic to animals, but she lived on that dairy farm all her life. All the dogs and cats had to be kept outside, and she could never help in the barn. But she did everything else. She was a full-time housewife, mother, nurse, bookkeeper, taxi driver, accountant, cook, washer, dryer, and ironer. She fixed shoes and sewed rips and holes in our clothing. She canned meats, vegetables, and fruits for the winter months. She also did most of the garden work, picked all the berries and fruits, made her own cream and butter, and baked cakes and pies.

Meanwhile, Dad literally lived outdoors in the fields or in the barn. Mom had to yell at him daily for breakfast, dinner, and supper, and to let him know when it was time to stop cutting hair or go to bed.

My mother always insisted my brothers and sisters and I clean our shoes before coming into the house. I always wondered why she was so persistent. One Saturday morning she said it was my turn to clean the floors. She gave me a broom, dustpan, mop, and bucket. After that day, I never had to be reminded about cleaning shoes again. In fact, I helped remind everybody else to clean their shoes or take them off before entering the house.

Mom's idol was the Blessed Virgin Mary. Mom had a soft heart, was a good referee, and had a great ear for music. She belonged to the PTA, the Catholic Daughters, the Red Cross, the Board of Elections, and the local sewing club. She was a band mother and a sports mom. She organized all family events. Mom had a daily calendar of birthdays and always sent a card. Rarely did she miss an event. We figured at one time that she had attended over two thousand outings or events involving her children. And then there was Dad, who avoided events. Unlike Mom, he was always an hour late. In fact, outside our kitchen window hung a large, old-fashioned church bell. Whenever Mom wanted Dad's attention, she'd start banging on the bell with a hammer. Soon after, Dad would appear from somewhere among the 185 acres or the barn.

Recently, as a tribute to Mom's enduring teachings, my four brothers and I were dining at a smorgasbord. Brother Bernard said, "Mom's not here. Let's eat dessert first."

After Mom and Dad returned from their honeymoon, family and neighbors treated them to an old-fashioned "belling." A belling usually took place during the middle of the night. Everybody had something to bang on to make a lot of noise. Bells, whistles, dishpans, kettles, dinner bells, and firecrackers can make a lot of commotion when in the hands of hundreds of people.

If you were home during the belling, you had to get out of bed and invite everyone in for a drink and food. If you were not home, your house was broken into and trashed with straw, hay, and feathers. Sometimes you got a hog-crate ride together in back of a wagon or truck. They were all a special tradition from way back when. Somehow, Mom and Dad got all versions.

Someone once asked Mom if she was ever worried about me getting hurt. She said no, "if his heart is in it, he'll be okay."

A COUPLE OF MOM'S FAVORITE SAYINGS

Letting the cat out of the bag is a whole lot easier than putting
it back in.

If you lie down with a dog at night, you'll stink like one in the
morning.

GROWING UP ON A FARM

I was born on the first day of spring in 1937, in the middle of
the Depression years and just before WWII, on our first farmhouse
east of Wooster. Mom and I had to be taken by ambulance thirty
miles to Mercy Hospital in Canton because of some birth complica-
tions. We were released some weeks later. By that time, I was king
of the nursery, weighing nearly twenty pounds! Everybody called
me Dicky. I hated Richard, but Dicky was worse. I like short names
like Bo, Bob, Jim, or Ike. Can you imagine always saying and spelling "Richard Phillip Schafrath"?

My first real injury was at age two. Mom was hanging clothes
on a clothesline out in our backyard, and I was playing in the grass
with my ball and bat. The ball rolled under the fence into an adjacent cow pasture, and I crawled under the fence to get it. I was
gored in the head by a cow thinking I was a threat to her newborn
calf. It took some forty stitches to sew the back of my head shut. After that, my excuse for doing something wrong was that I lost some
of my brain. That worked with some people, but never with Mom.

My second major mishap was at age four. My dog Biscuit and I
were walking along a nearby creek. All of a sudden I fell into a deep
water hole and panicked. Biscuit had to help me back to the bank
because I couldn't swim. I can still remember hanging on to him.
I never learned to swim and I am scared to death of water to this
day. Biscuit and I were inseparable. Whenever Mom couldn't find
me, she'd usually go to the second floor of the house and start looking out windows. We were surrounded by farm fields. She'd either

see my head or my dog's tail someplace through the wheat, oats, or high grass, and she'd come and get us. Someone shot Biscuit. He crawled back to our house. I held him in my arms until he died. The shooter said he mistook him for a deer. That experience hurt.

When I was six, we moved to the farm where Mom was raised. It was near a small burg west of Wooster called Jefferson. The house, built in the 1850s, was small with three rooms downstairs and three rooms upstairs. Downstairs consisted of a common gathering area and a kitchen/dining room with a stove at one end for cooking, boiling water, and heating. The stove burned wood or coal and was the only source of heat in the house. There was a pantry for storing potatoes, eggs, vegetables, and canned foods, and a third, smaller room for storing cooking supplies and drawing water.

Upstairs there were three small rooms, two of which contained a light bulb. There was also an attic with one bulb and no heat. We had one inside hand pump for water, but there were no indoor toilets or showers, no washing machine, no dryer, no television, no microwave, no refrigerator, and no freezer. All the boys slept in the attic in two beds. We sometimes slept up to five in a bed under a heaping pile of covers. I always joked that I never slept alone until I got married! To stay warm in the wintertime, you heated a soapstone on the stove, wrapped it in a towel, ran to the cold attic, and jumped under the covers with it. Somebody had to get up every two hours during the night to re-stoke the stove. If we forgot, we might find our clothes frozen stiff in the morning.

PLUMBING

Until I was a senior in high school, we had no indoor plumbing. Our toilet was located about a hundred feet from the house. This outhouse was a small, enclosed building with two seats side by side—a big one for adults, and a smaller one so that children would not fall through. For toilet paper we had a wooden box nailed to the wall filled with torn-out pages of catalogs, phone books, magazines, newspapers, and even corncobs. Since it was more convenient, the boys normally went behind a tree or bush. We had to clean the toilet drain area out with buckets every month. Boy, that was fun. It sure would clear your sinuses.

In the evening, just before dark, everybody went to the toilet. If you got up in the middle of the night, you had to carry a lantern or flashlight to see where you were going. Occasionally you would run into a skunk, raccoon, or fox. We did have a bedpan with a lid, the "slop pot," in the house in case of an emergency or sickness. Neighbors, family, and friends made sure everyone went to the bathroom before they visited the Schafraths.

Our two-room school also had outside toilets, one outhouse for boys and one for girls. The first regular toilet I used was at St. Mary's grade school when I was about ten or eleven.

As a prank, a few friends and I once borrowed a neighbor's outhouse when the family was not at home. It was Halloween night, and we took the outhouse to town in the back of our old pickup. We put it in the middle of the square in downtown Wooster. We even painted the neighbor's name and phone number on it. Luckily, we never got caught.

My family was really excited when we finally built our own indoor shower and toilet. At that time I was a senior in high school, and we all started to argue and fight for equal time. As a concession for a year or so, Dad and all us boys still went outside to the toilet most of the time.

The water pump in the kitchen sink was used constantly for drinking, cooking, washing dishes, washing clothes, and putting water in a washtub to take a bath. We usually got into a big tub full of water and washed our dirty bodies once a week, on Saturday night. We used the same water for everybody. The smallest kids went first. It was pretty dirty by the time I stood in the tub. That's why I loved sports—showers! The hand pump in the house had a sink built around it. You had to prime the pump to get it started. So each time before you stopped using it, you had to fill a jug with water to be ready for the next use. If not, you were up the creek without water. If someone happened to use or drink the water you put aside, you got mad! You had to go to the barn with a bucket for more water for priming. That pump was finally replaced by an electric powered unit when we got indoor plumbing.

Up to that time, we never were affected by power problems. Suddenly we were completely dependent on juice for everything to work properly—water, radio, TV, toilets, showers, stove, alarm clocks, refrigerator, freezer, etc. If the electric went off, we were in trouble. And it happened a lot, especially in stormy weather. We quickly learned to keep our flashlights ready, have gas-burning lanterns handy, and use only wind-up clocks.

Inside the barn we did not need electricity to function. We had spring water that ran continuously. A big cement trough was built for all the farm animals to enjoy fresh water day or night. We humans enjoyed it, too! Nothing tasted as good on a hot day as cool spring water coming from that spigot. We had a tin cup hanging on a nail near the trough for fifty years, and everyone drank from it. As far as I know, it was never washed.

Dad and I sometimes used the horse trough for bathing. We'd jump in and scrub off. It was a little cool, but it was better than the dirty water we had to use after everybody else had taken their dips in the same tub.

THE WAR

During WWII, Mom and Dad reached an unusual agreement with our church to house three German men who had deserted Germany to be in America. They stayed with us for about three months. We communicated with them mostly by hand signals. I was the great interpreter. They slept in our barn at night and helped Dad with his daily chores. They ate their meals with us at our house. Always smiling and happy, Mom washed their clothes once a week whether they needed it or not.

Because of the war, there was a lot of rationing of food, gas, clothing, sugar, and salt. I can remember more than one time standing behind the kitchen door in my nightgown listening to a potential robber trying to get in. I felt sorry for him if he succeeded. Mom would waiting for him, holding an ax, and I was armed with a broom. My heart was beating so hard that I thought it was coming out of my chest. Dad worked night shift so he could do farmwork during the day, so he was seldom home. We decided to get another dog, and that helped solve the lootin' problem.

RADIO SHOWS AND COMIC BOOKS

We had one radio in our house, but we seldom listened to because it was always cracking and popping. We heard news and weather during breakfast and a couple of radio shows before bed. We listened to country music stations as we did our chores. Dad always said our cows milked best to Hank Williams and Grandpa Jones. We had no radio in our car or truck.

Some of the radio personalities I still remember: Jack Armstrong, All-American Boy, Burns and Allen, Abbott and Costello, Amos and Andy, Fibber McGee and Molly, Jack Benny, sportscasters, Bill Stern and Mel Allen, the Lone Ranger and Tonto, Superman, the Shadow, Andy Griffith, Hank Williams, Tennessee Ernie Ford, Minnie Pearl, and Eddie Arnold. One of the first things I ever purchased was a transistor radio. I used to wire it to whatever I was riding—bicycle, car, truck, and tractor. The problem was, it usually only worked if the vehicle wasn't moving.

We never had a TV on the farm until I was out of high school. The first one that Mom and Dad purchased was a black-and-white RCA with a six-inch screen. The first TV I saw was at a small neighboring town four miles to our west, New Pittsburgh. It was in the window of a country store, and Mom and I would drive there and sit outside the window on a bench and watch some of the Cleveland Indians' 1948 games. At a neighbor's farmhouse I first saw shows with Ed Sullivan, Steve Allen, Perry Como, Jackie Gleason, Jack Benny, Fred MacMurray, Lucille Ball, Howdy Doody, Dean Martin and Jerry Lewis, Bob Hope, Bing Crosby, and wrestling matches with guys like Gorgeous George, Argentina Rocco, and Don Eagle. My mom, two uncles, and I even went to the Wooster Armory once to watch them wrestle live. The first thing I purchased with my $750 Cleveland Browns' signing bonus was a twelve-inch Zenith color TV. My wife Bonnie and I gave it to my mom and dad. It got three channels.

Everyone was crazy about comic books in the 1940s and '50s. I'd get them used from my Uncle Bob when he was finished reading them. They were the hottest things going and cost about ten cents each. I remember having hundreds in boxes before I left for college: Archie, Tarzan, Superman, Spiderman, Roy Rogers, Dale Evans, Gene Autry, Lone Ranger and Tonto, Dagwood and Blondie, Red Ryder and Little Beaver, and on and on. Mom gave them all away or burned them when I went to college. They probably would be worth thousands of dollars today.

I would go to the movies on Sunday afternoons as much as possible. The cost was twenty-five cents. Pop, candy, and popcorn were five cents each. An usher with a flashlight led you down an aisle to a seat. The movies always started with a cartoon followed by a newsreel of national and world happenings, and, last, the feature film. Lots of boys and girls went to the movies just to hug and kiss—which to me seemed like a waste of time.

My favorite movies featured Tarzan, Roy Rogers and Dale Evans, Gene Autry, Doris Day, Esther Williams, Dean Martin and Jerry Lewis, John Wayne, Gary Cooper, Bob Hope and anything that had American Indians!

Six of my friends and I would sometimes go to a local drive-in theater. Five would hide in the trunk so only two would pay. After awhile it stopped being fun. No one ever caught us, so we quit doing that.

PARTY LINES

Making a phone call was a lot of work. You had to crank the phone, ring for an operator, and then ask her to dial the number you wanted to call. Everybody in farm country had to do this in the 1930s through the '50s. Living in the country, we were one of twelve farm families on the same phone line. That meant that any one of twelve different homes could pick up the phone at any given time and listen to the conversations of any one of the other eleven who could use it. Seldom could you find the line free until after 11 p.m. or midnight. If you wanted to hear the latest gossip, just pick up the phone, kick your feet up, put your head back, and let the fun begin! Love affairs, arguments, fights, threats, and rumors—it was all there.

If there was a real emergency, you had to yell, "Emergency, please." Everybody would quickly hang up. You'd better have an emergency, though, because everyone would be picking up their phones to listen after a minute or so. It was impossible to call anyone at a prearranged time except between midnight and 5 a.m. I once told a girl at school I'd call her one evening, but I could not get through. She thought I had snubbed her and would not talk to me for days.

FOOD

Food—now there's an important subject! Food's on the table? Be on time, no exceptions! Breakfast was at 7 a.m., dinner (which was lunch) was at noon, and supper was at 6 p.m. We usually had visitors or extended family eating with us. There always was enough for one more person no matter how many people showed up, but rarely were there leftovers. If one of us brought a friend to the house, or if strangers stopped by before midnight, Mom would whip up something and make sure they ate a hot meal. Dad would pop popcorn so they could eat on the way home.

Guests had the first serving after Dad prayed. We had meat, potatoes, and lots of gravy at dinner and supper. We seldom used napkins—sleeves and undershirts worked better! We usually drank soup out of our bowls. A knife and fork were always in the pan of meat so you could help yourself. There was always a half-gallon jug of cold, fresh cow milk on the table. Again, help yourself. It would need to be refilled a couple of times a meal. During the summer, there also was a gallon jug of homemade iced tea or lemonade on the table. We always had pie, cake, and sometimes homemade ice cream. Just help yourself. It was not uncommon to see my dad eat a whole pie. He was six foot one and weighed about 185, but he could eat like a horse. He burned it all off in the fields. I was six foot three and weighed 210, and in high school a normal breakfast for me was a dozen scrambled eggs, some sausage, and a couple of bowls of bread, sugar, and milk, called "sop." A special treat was Mother's Oats (oatmeal), brown sugar, and cold milk. Boy, I loved food and plenty of it! I was told I had hollow legs since I never gained much weight.

We seldom ate out, but I remember one rainy Saturday evening my parents took all the kids to a place called the Smithville Chicken Inn. They had all the chicken you could eat for twenty-five cents a person. After about a half hour, I couldn't see my father across the table any more since the chicken bones were piled so high! When we went back the next rainy Saturday, we saw that the prices had doubled. The food was great, but we never went back because Dad was afraid the prices would be doubled again. The restaurant is still there today, but I'm not sure what the price of chicken is. I once asked Dad what he'd do if he inherited a million dollars. Without hesitation he said, "I'd keep on farming 'til I run out of money."

During the summer, haying and thrashing days were special. Just like the Amish, all the farmers worked together in the fields while their wives prepared the noon dinner. Wow, what a feast! I loved those times. The Amish still do this today.

Close to the barn was a springhouse, a small building where the spring water ran through before reaching the barn. We used it to keep food and drinks cool. Things like milk, melons, and other per-ishables kept longer in this shed. Dad made sure there were always big blocks of ice there. We even kept ice cream in there at times. Didn't last long though. Some culprit usually ate it.

Next to the springhouse was another small enclosed shed, the smokehouse. That's where we smoked, salted, and cured all of our meats after butchering. Things like sausages, hams, steaks, and ribs all hung on wires and hooks above a fire ring for smoking. Once the smoking process was finished, you had to be sure all entrances to buildings were completely secured. Every animal in the area was desperate to gain entry.

I always helped with the butchering, which was a big event for family and neighbors. It always occurred during the cold winter months. It was hard work but a lot of fun. Everyone brought their animals to be butchered for summer and fall food. There might be twenty to thirty people helping. If you got hold of the pig's tail, you could sneak up behind somebody and pin it on the back of their shirt or coat. Everybody enjoyed that. It was hard to kill an animal that you had fed and raised—look it in the eye and then shoot it. I did it once, but I couldn't do it again. One of us always had to chop the chickens' heads off if we wanted chicken to eat. That wasn't as bad. But I didn't like it either.

When I worked for a construction company, Mom would pack me a basket filled with sandwiches (eight or more). Fellow workers felt sorry for me and would share some of their lunches, too. I'd occasionally stop at a local Wooster restaurant, Keeney's, for more food. Sometimes I'd order everything on one side of the menu. The manager would give me two trays when I came through the door. People would freak out!

Later on, my wife Bonnie and I lived in an apartment across the street from another Wooster restaurant, the Coccia House. For a year I'd go over for a snack every night before bedtime. My usual order was full portions of spaghetti and ravioli and a pizza to go.

For late evening snacks while attending Ohio State, I would usually stop by a White Castle restaurant and get six six-packs of hamburgers to go (that was thirty-six hamburgers in all). Because of my eating reputation, Woody Hayes decided to take charge. For one quarter he had me learn table manners serving tables at a frat house.

To try and gain more weight when I played with the Browns, I entered eating contests all over the state of Ohio. I'd eat as much as it took to win. Pies, pancakes, hamburgers, hot dogs, eggs, pizza, watermelon—whatever my opponent wanted to try. I never lost.

CLOTHES

No one in our family ever purchased new clothes except as gifts. Dad would be given a new shirt or tie for almost every occasion, only he would not wear any of them for years. Things had to be broken in and used a few times by us before he felt comfortable enough to try them on. We kids loved breaking clothes in for him.

Dad had two closets with dozens of ties hanging on the doors. Bows were thrown into a dresser drawer. Most of these critters were from the Middle Ages, having belonged to his father and his grandfather. The other ties were all gifts. And they all looked the same—dark blue, black, brown, and wrinkly.

Every time there was something special going on in town or a family happening, Dad and his five boys each had to wear one of the ties. Dad was never too concerned about pictures that were taken, his theory being that the picture was always in black and white, so who could tell the difference?

For my senior class picture, I bought my own tie. The picture was in color, too!

Growing up, each of us boys had a suit and a sport coat. We never wore them except for picture-takings, weddings, or funerals. Mom always made sure when she got our clothes that they were about two sizes too large so we could "grow into them." But we grew right out of them fast. Mine were always too big or too small. Never just right! I'd give them to my brothers, who had the same problems. In high school I wore blue jeans everywhere. Blue jeans, T-shirts, and short-sleeved shirts. For farm work I wore bib overalls with no underwear, no socks, but always shoes. I wore bib overalls before they were in style.

Mom washed and ironed all our clothes on a washboard by hand and hung them to dry on an outside clothesline with wooden pins. We never heard of washers and dryers or dry cleaners. She also mended all rips and tears. She had thread and buttons to match any color. She once made dresses for herself and my sister Kathleen out of colorful farm sacks—yellow, blue, red, green, and orange. Actually, they looked pretty good, but for some reason they never quite caught on as a fashion item.

The men didn't take to the burlap feedbag clothes quite so well. One time Mom handed Dad and me brightly colored boxer shorts. Dad refused to wear them. He said they itched too much. So Mom said, "Okay, if you don't appreciate them, I'll give them to the neighbors." I don't know if they ever wore them because no one would ever say anything negative about a gift from Mom.

THE FIRST CAR

The first car our family owned was a Model-T Ford. We had to hand crank it to start the engine. You had to be careful because that baby would really kick when you first started to crank it. For some reason, all of the cars and trucks we owned after the Ford were Chevrolets. They had to be used Chevy's, too. Dad never trusted anything new.

When I was ten, I started driving Dad's truck to and from the fields, and in town to the Wooster Farm Equity. Dad accompanied me early on and talked about defensive driving all the time. After age twelve, I drove alone for farm-related work and to the Equity for fertilizer and grain supplies. I drove the car with Dad to church every Sunday from age ten on. Did anybody question it? Nah. Nobody gave it a second thought. Of course, most farm kids drove at an early age.

DAIRY FARMERS

My hat goes off to all dairy farmers. They are married to the job seven days a week, 365 days a year. Cows have to be milked twice a day or they will dry up. Dad always had Holstein (black and white) cows. We always milked them close to the same time, 6 a.m. and 6 p.m. On Sundays they had to wait an hour or so in the morning until we got back from church.

From age five to seventeen I milked cows by hand with my father. We each used a short, three-legged stool to sit on and a two-gallon bucket to milk into. When milking, you have to anticipate hazards—cow kicking bucket, cow stepping in bucket, cow swatting flies, splashing your hair with some loose poo. These things have a tendency to change the taste of milk. A good milking cow will give over two gallons of milk at a sitting. Dad always raced me milking. Of course, no one could beat him. His huge, wide hands, hard and rough as boards, wouldn't stop squeezing. He'd get going in a rhythm and not stop until the bucket was full. Occasionally he liked to squirt the milk from the cow into a cat bowl ten or twenty feet away or even into a hungry cat's mouth. The barn cats would actually sit in a line waiting for the squirts. If you were a visitor in the barn, watch out! You'd probably have some milk running down the side of your neck. One time Kathleen (I affectionately called her Yuk) wanted to help. Dad told her to get a bucket and stool and go to the eighth stall and milk, and she did. After about five minutes, she said, "Dad, this cow won't stand still, and it doesn't have things like yours. It's different." He started laughing. It was our bull!

TRACTORS

Our first and last tractor was an Oliver. Every farmer I've ever known never changes tractor models. If it's a Ford, it's always a Ford. If it's John Deere, then it's always John Deere. My dad had an Oliver for fifty years. My brother Ed, who purchased the family farm, still has an Oliver.

I did not like the transition from mules to tractors. Riding the slow "iron beast" was boring and monotonous. Growing up competing with my father, I always liked the manual labor part of farming. Besides, tractors were dangerous if you weren't paying attention. With horses, you could fall asleep working a field and they'd pretty much keep doing the same thing or stop. Also, they knew where the barn was to get you back home. The tractor was not as intelligent.

One day Dad had me on a tractor harrowing the field while he was with the mules planting corn. I fell asleep for a few seconds, and the tractor promptly looked for a fence to run in to. It tore down about fifty feet of fence before it stalled and was twisted up with the harrow and fence.

When everything stopped grinding and tearing, I jumped off and started running as fast as I could for our house. I knew Dad would be coming shortly. I started screaming, "Mom! Dad is going to kill me! Mom, help! I know he is going to kill me!" Before I could tell her why, sure enough, here he comes—long strides, knees high with his feet barely touching the ground. In his right hand is this long, black, mean-looking mule whip, and he's swinging it wildly over his head. Mom quickly steps between us and says to Dad, "Norm, calm down a second before you do something you'll be sorry for." Then she looks at me and says, "Now Dick, Dad is not going to kill you. Paddle you, yes. Kill you, no. But you are going to have to take some punishment."

Believe me, I never fell asleep on a tractor again!

A YOUNG FARMER

I belonged to 4-H and Future Farmers of America from age eight through high school. We helped a lot of local farmers with difficult problems. I planted hundreds of trees, picked up a lot of stones, and helped to tile and improve the farmland. I learned what crops grew best in hilly land and flat land, in sunny and shady fields. I learned how to test the different soil types, how to eliminate difficult weeds, and the importance of soil erosion control. Too much fertilizer, chemicals, and pesticides were dangerous to our health.

I always showed calves at the Wayne County fair. Dad helped me to pick the best calf, then train it to rope lead. I had my brothers' help as much as possible. They practiced a lot with the calf, trying to get it to follow a lead rope. Sometimes the calf was very stubborn. It would lock all four legs and refuse to move. At this point, we brought out the trusty "Ol' Oliver" tractor. A rope around the calf's neck and a steady slow pull was just what the doctor ordered. It only took a few seconds for the calf to decide to walk. Sometimes during the fair it would revert back to its old stubborn habits right at show time, and I'd have to act as normal as possible while dragging it before the judges' stand with all four legs locked. Needless to say, I never won many first-place ribbons, but I had fun. I slept beside my calf all week long and ate tons of junk food.

People have often asked what it was like growing up on a farm.

"What's so hard about it? You just milk a few cows and ride a tractor all day."

Well, on the farm there are always things to do. Typically, you get up at 3 a.m., milk twenty or thirty cows, then go and fetch fifteen to twenty buckets of drinking water from the well. Then you go out, chop down a tree, and cut it up into thirty or forty chords of wood and stack in a nice, neat pile. Feed a couple hundred chickens, gather ten dozen eggs for cleaning and weighing. Feed fifty to sixty goats, slop a hundred hogs, and zingo! You're ready for breakfast.

After breakfast things are simpler. Go out and fix the tractor. It'll take you about three to four hours. Then plow five or six acres of ground. After that you dig and dig and dig in the potato patch. When you've got about six bushels of 'em, you head off to pitch fifteen to twenty tons of hay. Go to the orchard and pluck twenty or thirty boxes of apples, and zingo! You're ready for lunch.

After lunch it really gets fun. Dig a drainage ditch around the first forty acres and put up a fence around the other forty. Hustle back to the house and churn about two hundred pounds of butter. Bed down about two hundred cows, then curry about a hundred horses, feed cats and dogs, and zingo! You're ready for supper!

Then take a break, rest five or six hours, and zingo! It's time to do it again.

BATTING STONES

Everyone should have a way to relax and get away from the real happenings in their lives. Mine was at our barnyard batting stones. Our outside barnyard was my dream land, my fantasy park, my therapy ground for thinking and relaxing. I visualized it as a ball field. Along one whole side of our barn was a driveway full of small stones. Each year Dad had stones put there by the thousands so the dirt driveway would not get muddy. I would hit stones by the hours into the barnyard with a beat-up old wooden ball bat. I was always pretending I was one of the 1948 Cleveland Indians, and I copied whether they were left- or right-handed. I would throw the stones up into the air with one hand and then hit them with both. I started doing this when I was about seven years old. I had marked off different areas of the barnyard for singles, doubles, triples, and home runs.

I'd get in a zone and bat nine-inning games for what seemed like hours. I would announce the players to bat. I pretended like I was the radio announcers Jimmy Dudley and Jack Graney. I pretended to be the crowd cheering each batter. The ultimate was to bat stones while actually listening to the Indians on my transistor radio. After each hit, I'd cheer or moan depending on whether it was a hit or an out. I had a barnyard full of fans. All the animals would stand, sit, or lay and watch—unless a stone would come at them, and they'd all scatter and bellow! My number-one fans were the mules. They honked at me a lot.

I'd go through two or three wooden bats a year. The last time I batted stones was in 1986, the day after my re-election to the Ohio Senate. A couple of years after both my parents passed away, all of us kids were dividing some old mementos, and I saw the last old beat-up bat I had used for batting stones. Lots of great memories. I wish I had kept it.

I also liked throwing a rubber ball against the side of the barn and catching it. One day at lunch, Dad said, "I had an idea after watching Dick throwing the ball up against the barn. Why don't we get a bucket of white paint—he can dip the ball in it each time before he throws. He could probably paint the barn in a day or so."

THE WOOD PILE

Each year we had a big pile of wood in our backyard. The pieces of wood were twelve or fifteen feet long, and they were stacked on end, leaning up against each other to form sort of an Indian teepee to stay dry. When we were ready to use wood, we'd cut these into shorter pieces to fit our stove.

One summer day, I was in the backyard throwing my ball high in the air and catching it. I missed one, and it bounced high and went right into the top of the woodpile. I climbed up and looked down. There was my ball down about three or four feet, sitting next to a seemingly quiet hornets' nest. I carefully stretched out, leaned down, and retrieved the ball, but the nest was not empty. I was stung a few times before I could scramble back to the ground, and suddenly it seemed like hundreds of angry hornets were after me. I sprinted for the barn and the cold water trough with hornets swarming after me, stinging every second. I dove into the trough clothes and all! I stayed under the water until the hornets left. I had been stung nearly a hundred times. I looked and felt horrible. My dad made me strip and packed me with wet mud. I was lucky. I was a sick boy for a few days. From that day on, I made sure my ball stayed clear of the woodpile.

BIRDING

Every farmer's barnyard had a large stack of straw piled outside of the barn when the wheat was thrashed. It was used all winter as bedding for the horses, cows, and mules, and later we would spread the soiled straw on the fields so the ground would be ready for spring planting. The animals would walk around the base of this huge straw pile, and over the weeks, they'd rub a big dent in it about five feet high. At night, birds would roost in the top of the "shelf" that was created.

We had a game called "Birding." With a flashlight and brown paper bag, you'd go around and reach into the top part of the straw and nab those birds while they slept. You could catch a bag full in a short period of time. We tried to see how many we could catch in fifteen minutes. After we counted them, we set them free. They'd usually go right back to the stack and roost.

DE-RATTIN'

In our dirt-floored chicken coops, rats would carve a city of tunnels about a foot deep and have the "life of Riley" eating chicken feed. So, about every month we'd have "Rat Night." We'd take all the chickens out of one chicken house and put them in another for the day. That night, all the neighbors would meet at the empty chicken coop at midnight. They'd be armed with empty feed sacks, ball bats, and four or five hunting dogs, as well as a dozen or so ten-gallon cans filled with water to pour down the holes. Everyone wore long pants and boots, and they made sure to stuff the ends of their pants into their boots. A scared rat up the inside of a pant leg could cause real trouble! We'd close the door and start de-rattin'! On a given night, we'd catch five or six dozen rats. We had designated places not worth mentioning to get rid of them.

WORK ETHIC

I'm fortunate to have been born and reared during the Depression and WWII years. It was kinda like we were living at the edge of a lot of new beginnings. America was proud and independent. Most families were blue-collar immigrants who stayed at the same job most of their lives. Agriculture and manufacturing was at its peak. A dollar was worth something. You were family. You knew who grandparents, aunts, uncles, and cousins were. People were friendly, helpful, and team-oriented.

At a very young age, my dad taught me the meaning of hard work, one that you can't find in the dictionary. He had this way of cocking his head with a smirk just before we'd go at it. No words were ever uttered or needed. Every kind of work we did became an immediate contest—bailing hay, shocking wheat, husking corn, pitching manure, chopping or sawing wood. Working with Dad was fun, competitive, and a challenge. No one could outwork him, but I'd try. We raced to see who could dress the fastest, eat the fastest; we'd race to the barn—sometimes with only one leg in pants or one shoe on. Milk cows the fastest. Gather eggs to see who could carry the most. I can't tell you how many we'd drop. Race to the hog trough with two buckets full of slop spilling all over our pants and shoes.

Dad hated change. He loved farming the old-fashioned way. He thought tractors were a sign of weakness. When I finally left for college, Dad had to change. He gave in to the modern way of farming, letting my brothers run the equipment while he lost himself in the task of taking care of his small animals in his own way

To this day, I often think back to those work games of competition. I can still see the determined expression on Dad's face as we cut away at the trunk of a large tree with a two-handed saw and thinking, *Tree, you don't have a chance with my dad!*

LEGS OF A MULE

Until I was approximately ten years old, we farmed like the Amish. We had four horses and two mules, named "Buck" and "By-Golly." Buck always was hitched on right side, By-Golly on left. That's the way they wanted to work. Dad plowed our garden in the fall with Buck. Then in the spring, Buck would pull a spring-tooth harrow to smooth the earth for planting. To get in good physical condition, I would sometimes put on the harness and pull the plow like Buck with my brothers hanging on to the plow. It built great leg power. I'd recommend it to anyone who wants to have legs like a mule. We planted and harvested by hand all our vegetables, potatoes, fruits, and popcorn. At harvest time, a lot of our neighbors would gather at each other's houses to help pick and can everything. This was our food supply for the winter months.

By-Golly was always on the left. Buck on the right. I was always riding By-Golly alongside Buck to and from the fields while Dad stood on the bouncing wagon, his cap flapping in the breeze. He would guide them with the reins in his hands and call out directions: "Gee" (go right). "Haw" (go left). "Giddy up" (start walking or trotting). "Whoa" (slow down or stop). "Back back" (while pulling on reins). Once in a while we'd both ride a mule—racing to a wagon in the field. Those were fun times—riding bareback or being pulled in sleighs, buggies, or buckboards.

In the wintertime, we always had some fun with horses pulling the sleigh, but when tractors came along, the horses were too slow, especially in the snow. We'd get feed sacks or inner tubes, tie them behind the tractor with a long rope, and ride back and forth across the fields by the hour until the tractor ran out of gas or Dad stopped us.

Buck had a bad habit of sitting down when Dad hooked him up to pull something heavy. By-Golly was no problem. When we purchased our first Oliver tractor, Dad couldn't wait for Buck to sit down. He didn't have to wait long. With a load of manure on the spreader, Buck sat down. Dad quickly fired up the Oliver and pulled in front of him, tossed a rope around his neck, and slowly started to pull. Buck slid on his butt about twenty feet before deciding to get up. His backside was starting to sting too much from sliding in the gravel. That was the last time Buck sat when it was time to pull.

Dad got rid of our horses after two of them got spooked one day while he was planting corn. Kathleen was riding on the corn planter with him. He stopped at the end of the field to fill up the planter's boxes with corn, fertilizer, and seed grain. A few seconds later, the two horses jumped across a ditch and scooted down the road with Sis hanging on to her seat for dear life! She fell off about a half mile later. Thank God she wasn't seriously injured—just a few cuts and bruises. I actually thought they made her look prettier, or at least tougher. Of course, Mom said I couldn't make fun of her for a month. Anyway, about a mile further, one horse fell down at a sharp curve and broke its leg. It was immediately destroyed. Then Dad sold the other three. We kept By-Golly and Buck for a few more years until we decided to do all the farming with Oliver tractors.

Dad said the mules were the hardest and smartest workers and had great endurance, but you had to be careful because they had stubborn streaks and were sometimes unpredictable.

Mules are very analytical. Their curiosity sometimes is mistaken for bullheadedness. You've got to convince the mule that what you want to do with him is not going to hurt. They look at every situation differently, and they're not real quick to jump into something they're not familiar with.

They're a lot more intelligent than a horse. They are stronger and better workers, they have good feet for rough terrains, and they're calm in dangerous situations. A horse can be ridden or worked until it dies, but not a mule. It simply looks out for its own welfare.

Give the mule some respect.

CHAPTER TWO

SCHOOL DAYS

A TWO-ROOM COUNTRY SCHOOL

My first school, Jefferson, had two rooms—one for first through fourth grades, and one for fifth through eighth grades. The school was located one and a half miles from our house. Mrs. Orr, our teacher, taught first- through fourth-grade classes, and her husband taught the next four grades. We always started school with the Lord's Prayer followed by the Pledge of Allegiance. Mom always packed sandwiches for my lunch with a thermos jug of milk. I carried them in a metal Roy Rogers lunch box. The forty students had to help Mrs. Orr with all her school chores. We swept floors, cleaned blackboards, washed windows, helped fire up the coal-burning furnace, shoveled snow, emptied garbage cans, changed light bulbs, and cleaned the outdoor toilets. Someone was always appointed to pull the school bell rope at start and finish of the school day. All students were expected to help each other to learn the basic school subjects. Teamwork.

One school game I remember was "Antonnee Over." I have no idea where the name came from, but you divided kids on two sides of the schoolhouse, then threw a rubber ball over the building. If your side caught the ball before it hit the ground, you would race to the other side and have one shot at trying to hit someone with the ball. If you did, they were on your side. In fifteen minutes the game was over. The team with the most players won. We also ran races, jumped rope, played stickball, hide-and-seek, and chicken-in-the-middle. We carried marbles and yo-yos for instant action, played softball in the summer, and went sled riding in the winter. We liked spelling bees, math games, playing the flute, and singing songs.

NUNS AND THE ALTAR BOY

I transferred to St. Mary's Catholic School in Wooster as a fifth grader because of the prayer in school controversy. I loved and respected St. Mary's. I saw my first movie there—how ironic, "The Bells of St. Mary's." I thought priests and nuns were sent to us by God and that they communicated with God daily.

The nuns were called Sister So-and-So. Each wore a long black dress and a habit to cover her hair. They never were allowed to show their skin except for their faces and hands. Also, they never showed any hair on their heads. As far as I knew, they probably slept in those outfits, if they even slept.

A priest was always called Father So-and-So. He was in charge of the church and school, said mass, gave confession, and visited the sick. He also dressed in a long black robe with a shirt and white collar. He had no more skin showing than a sister. He wore a tall black hat when he went outdoors. You could see his hair. Our priest, Father Harmon, had been at St. Mary's a long time. He had married my mom and dad and almost every one of my twenty-three aunts and uncles.

Prayer, respect, and obedience were a big part of my middle-school life. We were told that Catholics were God's special people and that they had a lot of special rules. No inter-religion marriages, no divorces, no abortions, no contraceptives, no personal bibles, no sex before marriage, no eating meat on Fridays (hurray, fish day), and no working on Sundays. You had to go to confession every Friday to tell the priest your sins before taking communion on Sunday. We were not allowed to miss church on Sundays—it was a mortal sin. We were taught to say the rosary as a family every night. We prayed especially for dead souls living in purgatory so they could get to heaven. All prayers and songs at church were said in Latin. I liked the tradition.

The three sisters I remember most were Sister Eileen, Sister Teresa, and Sister Anthony. Sister Eileen was a tough disciplinarian. To keep order, she always carried clickers and a ruler at her waist.

I received lots of nasty cracks on my knuckles from her ruler. She usually got everyone's utmost attention with her clicker. If not, she would grab you by the hair or ear and you'd stand and dance around in circles until she let go. In 1948 I got both a knuckle whack and an ear dance when a friend, Jimmy Carfellie, and I were caught listening to the Cleveland Indians' World Series game on a transistor radio in the back of her room.

Sister Teresa taught me the basic footwork for sports, especially boxing, basketball, and baseball. She also taught the boxing basics to Jimmy Carfellie. During the 1950s and '60s, Jimmy became a good heavyweight contender. If he had found the right trainer, I'm sure he would have had a championship fight.

Sister Anthony taught me Latin and how to serve the priest at mass on Sundays.

I was an altar boy server every Sunday until I graduated from high school. There were four masses every Sunday and I served at the one at 6 a.m. My father and I went to the early mass so we could do the farm chores when we got back home.

Dad always sat in the third row at church. His eyes would glaze over and close. I'd swear he was asleep, but on the way home he could recite the priest's sermon word for word. Under our altar boy robes we wore our regular clothes. People used to joke about my attire. They could see my bare legs under the robe when I knelt down and when I'd roll my pant legs up to my knees. Sometimes, when I was in a hurry, I wore different colored socks or no socks at all, and holes were always in my shoe bottoms.

Before going home, we'd always stop at somebody's house that Dad and Mom had heard were needy and give them some fresh eggs, milk, vegetables, and fruit to enjoy. Once in awhile when driving home we'd hit an unlucky rabbit or pheasant running across the road. We'd always stop (we had a sack in the trunk). It was a bonus for dinner time!

In the seventh grade at St. Mary's, a friend and I one day decided to take justice into our own hands against a boy who was constantly picking on a couple of girls we liked. Also, we watched him cheating one time on a test. We forged a note to him and signed Father

Harmon's name on it. The note said that Father Harmon heard he had done some bad things and expected him to come to Friday's church confessional at 3:30 p.m. and confess his sins. Father Harmon's confessional didn't start until 4 p.m., and since I lost the coin toss, I would be the priest and my friend would be on lookout in case Father Harmon or one of the sisters came in early. Sure enough, the culprit came at 3:30. I heard his confession and gave him a lot of penance to do for the next couple of weeks. But before I could leave the confessional booth, four more people also came to confess their sins, believing I was a real priest. Boy, was I nervous! I camouflaged my voice, heard their sins, and gave them rosaries to say. Thank God we were not caught! We could have been kicked out of school. No one ever knew. It is ironic I was awarded "outstanding student" in religion courses that year.

I didn't always perform like an altar boy. When my friends and I felt ornery, we'd put cow poo in a paper bag and go to a neighbor's house in the evening. We'd go to a place with the lights on so we knew someone was home. We'd set the bag on the doorstep, light a match to it, ring the doorbell, and run like mad! Then we'd hide in the bushes and watch someone get stinky feet stomping the fire out!

Close to my Grandparents' farm east of town were a few small houses referred to as "Shantytown." Located next to Shantytown were two railroad tracks—they might still be there. At about age ten, a kid from Shantytown and I dared each other to dig a space under the tracks between the rails, lie down, and let the train run over us. We decided the best plan was to dig the holes just beyond a big curve at Gramps's farm so we could hear the train coming but not see it. We each picked a track to dig our hole under the wooden trusses and had just enough space to lie on our backs and look up. No one would know which track the train was on until it was on top of us.

A couple of weeks later on a Sunday afternoon, I was supposed to be at the local movies, but we were at the railroad tracks in our spaces. It was exciting as heck! After about an hour or so we could hear a train approaching the curve. The ground was shaking, the whistle was blowing, and the tracks were clicking and clacking. Hot dog! It was on my track going right over me! It seemed like an eternity before it finally passed. Most of the time my eyes were closed and I was saying bits of the rosary. It was not a smart thing to do. I've had some bad dreams about it since.

TRAPPER

The only time I recall missing school was when I thought I'd get rich becoming a trapper. One evening I carefully laid out six traps along a creek. Early the next morning I was checking for my beaver when I ran across one angry skunk. As hard as I scrubbed, the smell still stayed with me. Mom took me to school an hour late. I was directed to the principal's office. He got one whiff of me and said, "Dick, please take the rest of the day off." That was the end of my trapper experience.

BASEBALL

During the summer months, I played as much baseball and softball as I could. Dad would never let me stop working in the fields until about fifteen minutes before game time. In two minutes I'd be on my bike racing for town. When my teammates saw the bike coming, they'd yell, "Here he comes," and the umpire would yell, "Play ball."

During the 1940s, my friends and family played a lot of ball games on Sunday afternoons in the cow pasture. Dried-up cow and horse d dung was used for bases. Nobody had to sit on the bench and watch. Everybody played. We divided teams up equally mixing boys and girls. No umpires, no coaches, no special uniforms. Boy, that was baseball! We would play games until it was too dark to see. I always had a ball in my hand. I carried it everywhere hoping I could find someone to play pitch and catch. My uncles taught me to throw, catch, and hit.

Later on I played on every ball team I could find in Wooster. Slow pitch, fast pitch, whatever. One summer I played on three teams. I would play any position, but my favorite was catcher. I loved blocking the plate! The trouble was I didn't always have the ball. The umpire would say, "Schafrath, you have to let the runner score." I loved to run the bases. I always slid headfirst—Pete Rose style, but before Pete did it!

As a pitcher, I was a little wild. I threw only fast balls. No one ever taught me to throw a change up or curve. My shoes never fit right, so my heels were always hurting. I had what they called "Joe DiMaggio tender heels." The coaches and umpires would occasionally stop the game to correct mistakes and give all players some fundamental advice.

Baseball was my first love. I also ran track, and I asked the coach if I could just come to the track meets and play baseball everyday. We tried it for awhile, but it caused too many problems, especially when ball games and track meets occurred on the same day.

I was named All-Ohio Catcher my senior year of high school. I was offered a minor-league baseball contract with the Cincinnati Reds. I have one regret: that I didn't give pro baseball a try.

BASKETBALL

During eighth grade I got to play a few games in the local YMCA basketball league. I was exposed to the sport as a sixth grader. The sisters were our teachers and coaches. I loved banging into opponents. My uncle Don Starr gave me a pair of used tennis shoes to play in. Sister Teresa insisted I learn to shoot foul shots underhanded, Wilt Chamberlain-style. I even shot like that throughout my high school career. All outside shots were two-handed. I never saw a jump shot until I got to high school. I still thought you should shoot all long shots two-handed.

At home I took a wooden potato basket, cut the bottom out of it, and nailed it up on the wall at one side of our barn floor. Uncles Tom and Don Starr came through again and bought me a used basketball. I practiced when I could find time, usually on a rainy day or late in the evening.

After dark you had to drive a car up to the barn door and leave the headlights on so you could see to shoot. Later on Dad let me put a light bulb in that part of the barn, but it was far from playing in a real gym. For one thing, you couldn't do lay-ups because you'd run smack into the wall. If it wasn't the wall, there were stairs next to it, and you had to be careful not to go flying headfirst down them. Close to where you took the ball out-of-bounds was another hole in the floor where we threw down hay bales to feed the cattle. Many of my opponents disappeared down that hole.

In high school basketball it seemed I was always in foul trouble. Even though I averaged about twelve points a game, I fouled out of almost every game. I liked hitting too much. I played center and once scored a high of twenty-eight points in a game.

My first varsity game was as a sophomore, when I played the reserve game. Afterwards I learned I was to dress for the varsity game, but I was so excited that I forgot to put my trunks on under my warm-up suit. When I stripped off my long sweatpants and ran into the game, I could hear all of my teammates yelling. All I had on was my jock strap! I had to race back to the dressing room for trunks. I missed nearly four minutes of the first varsity game I ever played.

One night in the early 1950s we had a horrible snowstorm. The next day we were to play a tournament basketball game at Canton. The school bus could not run the country roads because snow drifts were five to six feet in some places. But the main highways were open. It took Dad and me two hours to make it to a spot where my coach had agreed to meet us and drive me to the game. When we met him, my clothes and shoes were soaked. He let me wear some of his clothes to the game. I know I looked like a clown, but I had a good night. I scored twenty-six points, and we won the game.

As a senior, I once played a game against a talented young freshman. I ran him into a wall a couple of times in the first quarter just to let him know I was there. I could tell he had a good future. He was to become a star at Ohio State University and a great coach for Indiana University. He was Bobby Knight of Orrville, Ohio.

BOXING

I loved to watch and read about boxing. Sister Teresa taught me the basics: keep your arms up, elbows in, be on your toes, keep feet moving, keep jabbing, and protect face and ribs. No round-house swinging. It came in handy because I can still remember when another kid at school sucker-punched me in the stomach for a big laugh. After I was able to breathe again, I leveled him with three quick jabs and a right hook. An Industrial Arts teacher in high school by the name of Mr. Spangler also worked with me at developing better boxing techniques. My favorite fighters were Rocky Marciano, Joe Lewis, and Sugar Ray Robinson. I could pick up Marciano, Lewis, and Robinson fights on my transistor radio late at night. Later on, it was a great thrill to meet in person Cassius Clay (who later changed his name to Muhammad Ali), Floyd Patterson, Smokin' Joe Frazier, and Pete Rademacher.

I finally boxed some live rounds for real in 1959 while serving in the United States Air Force basic training camp at Lackland near San Antonio, Texas. It helped me to get out of K.P. duty, but I got my butt kicked a few times by some good fighters. Two-minute rounds felt like an eternity when you're breathing hard and have not trained. After three rounds, I could not hold my arms up to punch or protect my face and body. My opponents used me as a punching bag, and I could hear Sister Teresa saying, "Stick with the dishes, Dick." I decided washing dishes wasn't so bad after all. Maybe it took a little longer, but it did not hurt as much.

RUNNING

I loved to run, and as a youngster my dad would often race me to and from the fields where we were working. I could never beat him. He had long strides and good endurance. He taught me to work hard, to work through pain, and to make work fun. Although there comes a point when your body says, "I quit," you can train your mind to say, "I'm not dead yet, I can still go on." One more step, one more play, one more minute, just keep pushing! It's up to you to overcome the pain of those negative thoughts and never quit. Most professional athletes have learned to do it. Lots of average people become heroes doing the impossible by never giving up. My dad always said, "As long as you can feel the pain, you know you're not dead!"

I always wanted to be like Jim Thorpe, who as a youngster beat his bus running to school. One day, like Thorpe, I raced my school bus five miles from our farm to school at Wooster and beat it. Of course, it had to keep stopping to pick up students. I ran track as a freshman and a sophomore in high school. I set a school half-mile record at the time, but I loved team sports better. The toughest part of track was to do a lot of running, then walk five miles home. I participated in four events: the half-mile run, the mile relay, the shot put, and discus. Still I couldn't get my shoes to fit right. My heels were always sore. Sometimes in practice I ran in my socks on the cinder tracks.

ROY BATES

I never did have a chance to play against my idol, Coach Roy Bates, and his outstanding Chester Huskies. I listened to them play as often as I could on the radio. Seemed like the varsity never lost. His freshman and reserve teams had 212 wins and no losses. They were the pride of Wayne County. I also learned that their players went to their high school gym year-round to practice on their own. Would that have been great!

Coach Bates was elected into the Ohio High School Hall of Fame as a coach in both basketball and baseball. He won the state championship in both sports and had more combined wins than any coach in the country. He won over 90 percent of his games. Later on he was also named for the third time to the High School Hall of Fame as an official. What I wouldn't have given to play for him! While I was a senior at Wooster High, he had an up-and-coming star eighth-grader named Dean Chance. He only lost one game in his high school career and went on to become a Cy Young Award winner in the major leagues. Once I heard Yankee pitching great Whitey Ford say that slugger Mickey Mantle hated to bat against Dean. Dean was a farm boy like me. He was also a great basketball player who led his team to a state championship. Dean pitched for the Angels, Twins, and Indians. He was once quoted as saying, "The reason Schaf and I were athletes, we either played sports or we stayed home and milked cows and worked the fields. When we had a ball game, we got to relax for a couple of hours."

FOOTBALL

I never saw a football game until I played in one. I heard games over the radio in the 1940s—Notre Dame, Ohio State, and the Browns. I was six foot one, 175 pounds as a freshman in high school, and I was six foot three, 210 pounds as a senior. I played fullback and middle linebacker. I never lifted weights and I was never timed in the 40-yard dash, but I suspect I ran between a 4.7 and 4.8.

My first physical was given to me on the farm by our veterinarian. Between the calves and pigs, Dad asked him to check me out, too. The vet said, "He's okay," and then signed a piece of paper for me to give to the football coach. It consisted of things like, could I see lightning? Yes. Could I hear thunder? Yes. Point left, point right. Say "Ahhhhhh." Okay, you pass.

At my first football practice, Coach Gene Coleman had a tradition where all the players had to sprint through a portion of a nearby city park that was loaded with trees. That was the way he selected his players. The guys who hit the trees were linemen. The guys who missed them were the backs. I didn't miss too many trees, but Coach noticed I seldom fell down, so he made me a fullback.

I'd never had a shower before I played football. After my first practice, when the coach said, "Hit the showers," I went in the shower room with my uniform on! Luckily, one of my teammates sent the coach over. He explained to me that a shower worked better with clothes off. I loved that hot shower. So I went out for basketball, track, and baseball. And my dad could never understand why I loved sports.

A good high school friend, Cy Morgan, invited me to stay overnight at his home once. Cy's family had a beautiful home in Wooster. Before going to bed that night, Mrs. Morgan handed me a big, soft towel. I thanked her, and when she left I asked Cy what it was for. That's for your shower in the morning. Okay. I didn't want to lose it, so I slept with it.

Morning came and Cy says, "Okay, Schaf, your turn—bathroom's yours." It was the first time I'd ever showered in a real live house. I had my towel. I put it on the counter, opened the curtains, and there it was. The curtains were white, dry, and clean, and I thought they were to stay that way. It took a few moments to get the water going right. I really enjoyed the shower, but water was going everywhere. A few minutes later I turned the water off and wondered what to do—boy, this is a messy experience. I used two more towels to wipe it up, but those shower curtains were still dry and clean!

I had excellent coaches and good linemen blocking for me in high school. I was fortunate to be named captain of our team during my senior year and All-Ohio for my junior and senior years.

After my senior year, I was picked to play in the high school All-Star game in Mansfield. That was an amazing experience. It was the first time as an athlete I stayed away from home. We roomed at the Mansfield Leland Hotel for a week. I practiced and played with some great athletes. It was 1955, and the coach was Mel Knowlton from Alliance, Ohio. Our side won 26-13. The Ohio All-Star Classic started in 1948 with Frank Leahy of Notre Dame fame as the first coach. Many great coaches have coached this game over the years.

During the 1940s, football uniforms weren't designed to fit skintight. And it only took five minutes or so into the game for my pants to become baggy and loose from all of the sweating. It didn't help that I was not allowed to drink water to keep my weight up. More on that later.

In one game, a defensive back was hanging onto the back of my baggy pants when my belt broke. The pants slid down to my ankles, making me trip and fall, and also revealing some skin. Coach Coleman made me go to the locker room and change my pants. When I got back to the field, I apologized to him. He said, "Aw, forget it, boy," with a grin on his face. He added, "That was the best showing you've had all year! Now get back in there and do it again!"

It was tough getting used to all the equipment—leather helmets, girdle pads, elbow pads, shoulder pads, rib pads, knee pads, plastic jock, thigh pads, and shin pads. I had to carry my practice uniform home with me if I wanted it clean. My poor mom would faithfully wash it by hand and dry it over our stove before morning.

Besides playing fullback and middle linebacker, I punted, kicked off, and helped return kickoffs. Wearing a leather helmet with no face mask and having no mouth guard, I lost eight teeth in high school. My nose was broken three times, and I had a lot of concussions. I would constantly get hit and see stars. I never tried to run around tacklers. It was much more fun to try and run over people or hit them head-on. And the leather helmet did not cushion the hits very much.

I was knocked out in one high school homecoming game but managed to stay on my feet. I stayed in to play several series. I knew the numbers and responded accordingly. They only took me out of the game when I went to the opponents' huddle. My teammates Cy Morgan and Tiny Conaton helped dress me after the game and then took me to the homecoming dance. They finally had to call my mom and say, "Mrs. Schafrath, you better come and get him. He's not normal. He doesn't know who he is." I didn't gain consciousness until about nine o'clock the next morning. Nobody thought of taking me to the doctor, hospital, or anything. I had work to do, and my dad, counting on me to husk corn, shook me awake. Dizzy and weak, I got up and helped him all day.

On the farm I used to practice kicking a lot, punting over the telephone and electric wires, then getting the ball and doing it over and over again. Jim Thorpe and Vic Janowicz inspired me to practice dropkicking in the cow barn every evening while the cows ate and were milked. As a matter of fact, I became pretty good at it. Never could convince my high school coach to try it in a game, though. I wanted to kick extra points like my hero, Lou Groza, but Leo Hanson, our halfback, got to because his family purchased a hard, square-toed kicking shoe for him. But truthfully, he was more accurate.

SODA POP

I never tasted soda pop until I was in high school. While walking home from high school football practice one evening, I stopped at a filling station. I discovered the owner was a great sports fan. He sold candy, cigarettes, chips, and cold pop. He made a deal with me. For every football and basketball game we won, I would get two pops. For every baseball game where I got a hit, two pops! I'd chug them straight down out of those cold glass bottles without taking a breath. Coke and Hires Root Beer were a toss-up. Boy, they were good! If I had a nickel, I'd always buy one more to nurse the rest of the way home.

THE NO-WATER RULE

I always had a problem maintaining and gaining weight during my playing career. During my football days, I'd lose fifteen to twenty pounds of liquid during a practice or game. After some games at Ohio State and with the Browns, I'd cramp up because for some reason the coaches never allowed us to drink water. I'd be so dehydrated that the doctor had to pack me in ice and feed me intravenously for awhile to stop my cramping. It helped get liquid back into my system very quickly.

The trainers would also force salt tablets down my throat. Dr. Murphy, OSU's team doctor, used my experiences for getting Ohio State and the Big Ten to change their thinking about drinking water. Everything finally changed during the mid-1960s. Water everywhere. But for many years, coaches wrongly enforced the no water rule.

(When I got to the Browns, it was the same thing—no water—until 1970. In the huddle during time-outs we'd pass around a towel to wipe the sweat off our faces. They called it the "healing towel."

After everybody wiped their faces, whoever was desperate enough would suck on it. All my career, high school, Ohio State and with the Browns—no water allowed! I sucked the towel.)

CARS AND DRIVING

The day I turned sixteen, at 8:30 a.m., my mom and I were standing first in line for me to take my written driver's test. At 9:30 a.m., I had passed the mental exam and was taking the driving part. Before noon I was legal. All in less than three hours,

I had some country friends who lived close to my Grandma and Grandpa Schafrath's farm east of Wooster. When I was sixteen, they let me drive their race cars during the summer in about a dozen local demolition derbies under the name "Bull Schaf." One car was blue and one was black, and those were the colors I was after most of the events—when I got crunched and sometimes a little shaken up. My parents never knew about this chapter in my life, but it prepared me for some hits I would take later on.

One cold, snowy, Saturday night, I drove the family car to town to see a Tarzan movie. When I got out of the movie two hours later, there was a blizzard in progress—a real white-out. I decided I'd better head straight home. The first mile was not too bad since the road graders were working hard to keep up with the falling snow. But as I started down the final three-mile, hilly, dirt part of the road to our farm, I sensed real trouble. Some of the drifts were already two or three feet high. I could barely see the telephone and electric poles lining the road. I was driving on memory and instinct, knowing that if I stopped, I was stuck. Suddenly I was gobbled up and sucked into a ditch. I couldn't move the car and couldn't get out the door. I had to crawl out the window. Mom always had a cap, gloves, and boots in the trunk, just in case of emergency. I grabbed a few things and took off walking toward home. It took me about three hours to go two and a half miles. I was freezing, soaked, and exhausted.

As soon as I thawed and dried out, Dad decided we had to get the car off the road before the road graders got to it. We bundled up, hitched Buck and By-Golly, and headed down the road, riding the sled as much as we could and walking the rest of the time. Dad pulled the mules half the time. The snow was as high as their legs. We reached the snowbound car and somehow pulled it a few feet off the road into a farmer's field before going on to church for 6 a.m. mass. Counting us, there were six parishioners and the priest in attendance. Buck and By-Golly both waited outside, of course.

We got home at 10 a.m. and helped finish the chores that my brothers and sister had started. We slept good that night.

STUPID STUNT

I liked pretending I was Roy Rogers or Gene Autry—always trying to board a horse or mule with a quick run and hop on from the rear. It was not as easy as it looked in the movies, and I had a lot of real bad falls. If I could have stayed with it a few more years and grown another six or more inches, I'm confident I could have made it to Hollywood, at least as a stunt man.

I practiced a lot in the barn to be a rodeo man. I learned to rope a calf in quick time, throw it down and speedily tie its feet just like they did in the movies. After awhile the calves got smart and lay down before I'd throw them down! That took all the fun out of it. Who said animals aren't smart?

My junior year in high school was the last time I rode a horse bareback. I was helping an uncle bale hay all day. When we quit for supper, I decided to unhook one of the horses and ride him bareback to the barn. I was used to riding without a bridle and saddle, but not on a strange horse. He was really flying towards the barn and I was enjoying the ride when I saw a potential problem ahead. We were fast approaching the barnyard area, and this stallion had no intention of slowing down despite my efforts to convince him otherwise.

The horse was galloping out of control toward the barn, silo, and wooden barnyard fence—all tied together and closed. Just before the fence area, he put his head down and came to a complete stop. Even though I had a hold of his mane with both hands, the rest of my body flew at the fence, and my legs hit the silo. I was knocked out for a few seconds and my left knee was completely numb. It was not broken, but the nerves were all crushed. Luckily, I could still walk.

I never could run quite the same again. That year I had water on the knee that had to be drained constantly. I never told my uncle, family, or coaches what happened. I brushed it off as a football injury. I was so stupid to do what I did. I never thought I'd be normal again. I learned to deal with the pain the rest of my life. Michigan coach Bo Schembechler once said, "I don't care if a player can play with pain I want to know how well he can play with pain."

DATING

I dated very little in high school. Playing sports and walking home five miles every night did not offer me many opportunities. Besides, I was too bashful to even talk to girls. There were other problems, too: no wheels, no money, no phone. Not too many girls liked riding on the back of my Schwinn bike.

When I did go out, it was either with Uncle Bob on a double date or with Mom driving us. Mom was something else, too. She'd give me three minutes to walk a girl to the door and say good-bye. Then she'd start honking the horn. Another I didn't date much was my coaches demanded their players all be home at 10 p.m. on weeknights and 11:30 p.m. on weekends.

My first kiss was in the eighth grade. A bunch of us were playing Spin-the-Bottle when somehow it stopped on me. The girl, Carol Quinlin, was real cute but aggressive. She kissed me hard for only about ten seconds, but it seemed an eternity! I got so embarrassed and upset. I ran outside, got on my bike, and raced home.

During the ninth grade I was asked to go double-dating to a ballroom big band dance. I agreed without ever having danced before. I had watched people moving together but had no idea what their feet were doing. The next day at school I asked a beautiful classmate, Barb Kelly, if she'd teach me a few steps. She said okay, but she didn't know much either. We both had some fun—trying. I can't remember if there was music or not, but I did get the knack of counting as I was stepping.

We discovered most music has no more than five beats. Any dummy can count to five. Trouble is my feet and brains are not attached!

During my junior year, I had my first date for the high school prom. Her name was Becky. I had to buy her a corsage. Since I lived in the country and my grandparents and uncles lived in the city, we made out the order together a week early, and they picked up the flowers for me on dance day. As a practical joke, my uncles took the flowers out of the box and hid them, leaving only the greens and ribbons. When I opened it to look, I said, "Boy, Grandma, that corsage looks pretty cheap to me." They all howled and roared with laughter. I once had a date with a pure-blooded Comanche Indian girl. I met her at our local fair and asked if she would like to go to a movie sometime. She said she would give me her phone number and told me where she lived.

I always had a fascination with Indians from cowboys and Indians stories. They were some of my biggest heroes, especially the Indian chiefs.

When I came to pick her up, I went inside to meet her parents. I noticed they weren't dressed like storybook Indians. I didn't see any tomahawks, bows and arrows, or Indian headdresses, but I did see some guns on the wall.

Her dad was short and direct when he spoke. He said he knew who I was. "You're Mr. Schafrath. Be careful what you do tonight with my daughter. She is my princess and I remember faces. I expect her home by 10:30." I hardly touched her hand all night. She was a very nice girl, but I was scared to death of her father. I could see him in the doorway with a scalping hatchet. I had her home at ten o'clock. In the car she asked if we could do some kissing. I said definitely not on the first date. I asked her one question that she thought was very funny. I said, "At what age do you become a squaw?" She laughed out loud. I never saw her again.

In the beginning of my junior year I was seated next to this classy, good-looking girl named Millie Conrad, and something weird happened. I was talking to her and suddenly blurted out, "Millie, would you go to the homecoming dance with me?" Lo and behold, she said, "Okay." At our recent fiftieth high school reunion, she still remembered our date.

She remembered me acting a little strange at the dance. Every once in awhile, I'd jump up and hop around in circles clutching my thigh area and moaning. What she didn't know was that I kept getting muscle spasms from playing football. She was glad I was able to explain my behavior, even if it was fifty years later. We had a good laugh.

BONNIE

Also during my junior year, I noticed a real sharp challenge—a special girl in my class. I asked Cy Morgan who this chick was. "Bonnie Flickinger, sister of senior football teammate Larry, the meanest, toughest hombre on the team." She seemed just the opposite—quiet, independent, and extremely confident. Not easy to get close to. Her father had left her before she knew him, and because of that, her mom didn't trust men. Also, she was Lutheran and didn't like Catholics.

Bonnie was class secretary and didn't much care for sports. She walked a mile to school every day, back and forth from their rented apartment. Since I didn't talk much, we only said "Hi" a lot in the hallways. She was a challenge, and I was not doing very well. She got tired of waiting for me to ask and went to the prom with the best-looking guy in the school.

One day our history teacher, Don Welsh, confronted me concerning my snail-paced effort. He said, "I know you'd like to date Bonnie. Everybody in school knows. She knows, too, and I promise you she won't bite. Say something more than 'hi' and she might talk. Try animals, farming, military, babies, eating, anything."

Six months had passed when finally, one day, perspiring and nervous, I broke the ice: "Hey Bonnie, would—" "Yes," she said without letting me finish the sentence. We had a date to go to the movies. No kissing or holding hands. She was not impressed with athletes, sports, or kissing. Still I found her very attractive and interesting. Her mom said no to going steady, since all men were after was sex.

The senior homecoming game was the breakthrough. I was captain of the team. She was the homecoming queen. At halftime, in front of all the fans, we had a nervous kiss. Wow, was that nice! I couldn't wait for the dance afterwards. Unfortunately, I was knocked out in the second half of the game and never saw her again that weekend.

A few weeks later I got up the courage to ask her for another date. She accepted and to the movies we went. I was very nervous thinking about whether I should try to hold her hand or kiss her, especially with my limited experience. My thoughts even went back to playing Spin-the-Bottle. Bonnie made it easy. She avoided getting close to me all evening. But at her doorstep when I was saying goodnight, and before Mom could blow the horn, I gently pulled her to me and kissed her on the lips. We kissed for a minute or so. She finally pushed me away and said, "Wow, Big Boy, where'd you learn to kiss like that?" I said, "Siphoning gas out of tractors."

For three or four years, until I was a junior at Ohio State, Bonnie and I saw each other whenever I drove home. It wasn't easy. Her mom had moved and they were now living forty miles away in Canton, Ohio.

By 1957 we were in love and planned to get married the next summer. But four weeks before the team was to play in the Rose Bowl, we decided to use the trip as a partial honeymoon. (Coach Woody Hayes made sure it was very limited and partial.)

WOODY HAYES RECRUITS MY PARENTS

I had excellent teachers and coaches throughout my first twelve years of schooling. I was an average student. I never had to do any homework. Either I finished it in study hall or the teachers didn't give me any. They knew I did not have time to study at home. All my spare hours were spent working at chores on the farm or playing sports. Plus there was a lot of commotion from Dad cutting hair in the evening, and there was only one dim light bulb in the attic to read by. Abe Lincoln, I wasn't. There was no way I was going to carry books five miles home after practice. At least, that's what I told myself.

Like my dad and the Amish, I knew the basics and was ready to move on with life. High school I tolerated, But in 1955, I had to make a decision because I was graduating from high school in a few weeks. Was it going to be football or baseball? I certainly was not interested in college. None of my relatives ever went to college. But if I didn't go, my mother wanted me to be a priest. My father wanted me to come to my senses and start farming. The simplest thing would be to sign a baseball contract and head south. Also, sometimes I was tempted to bypass everything and be a marine. I batted a lot of stones thinking about my future that spring and summer.

But Woody Hayes recruited me for Ohio State University during my junior and senior high school years, and he was persistent. I had gone to Columbus three or four times during those years where I was treated to shrimp cocktails, steaks, and other fancy foods. Woody's wife Anne was always great to me. Staying at the Hayes's home was an experience. The doorbells and clocks constantly going off to a steady stream of different Ohio State fight songs. Having an All-American Heisman Trophy winner by the name of Howard "Hopalong" Cassady and his wife, Betty, giving me personal tours of the campus was pretty persuasive. And being in the locker room before and after Buckeye games didn't hurt either.

A local attorney named Hank Critchfield took a liking to me. He was a former star football player in high school and college and played a short time for the Canton Bulldogs, a professional football team. He took me and Cy Morgan on a whirlwind tour of other colleges. It was the first time I was out of Ohio, and I got homesick real quick. We were in Kentucky, West Virginia, Tennessee, Texas, Oklahoma, Kansas, and Indiana. At first, my parents and Coach Leahy wanted me to pick Notre Dame. The only problem was that Mr. Leahy retired the year I graduated and his replacement, Terry Brennan, never called me. One place I really liked was the University of Kentucky and its coach, Blanton Collier. Lexington was not too far from Ohio. There Coach Collier said I could play fullback and middle linebacker. I would stay someplace at the famous Calumet horse farm, have a car to drive, and receive some spending money each month. It was almost too good to be true. Blanton even sent an assistant to the Wooster area for a week to help Dad on the farm and make sure I was signed to go to Kentucky.

Woody Hayes was monitoring everything daily and finally decided he'd had enough. He arrived at the farm the next Sunday. He went to church with the whole family and helped Mom cook lunch. He spent time with Dad at the barn talking about the chickens, pigs, and cows. He never said a word to me. Two hours later, he shook hands with Dad, kissed Mom on the cheek, and drove out the driveway. I came into the house a short time later and said, "Boy, Mom, I'm not very impressed with Woody Hayes and Ohio State." Mom looked at me, pounded her fist on the table and said, "That's okay, Dick, you're going to go to Ohio State!"

It made no difference that I had no interest in college. Woody had charmed my parents. When Woody recruited, he looked for discipline, loyal parents, and hard-working, responsible kids. He recruited boys on their attitude and their potential. He liked linebackers and fullbacks since he could convert them into any position. But I know I got my shot because of Mom and Dad. I remember one thing Woody said to me early on that has always stuck with me: "Son, be good to Ohio and Ohio will be good to you." After more than 50 years, I can assure you he was right.

Woody Hayes understood and respected farm people for their hard work ethics, toughness, dedication, loyalty, discipline, dependability—all ingrained farm characteristics. He was born and raised in neighboring Tuscarawas County, a rural, sparsely populated farm area. Like most farmers, he preferred to sit at the kitchen table with guests rather than in the living room.

Coach Hayes would get close with parents like they were relatives. I never realized just how much of a role he would play in my life and just how much time I would spend with him in the years ahead. He won over my parents big time.

So in August 1955, I left home to start my new life. Mom was hugging me and crying, and Dad was trying to give me words of support: "Remember son, give 'em all ya got!"

LETTER FROM WOODY

The Ohio State University
Department of Physical Education
June 10, 1955

Dear Dick:

I have a feeling that you enjoyed your trip to Columbus, but I want to tell you that you could not have enjoyed it as much as we did. Having you and Bonnie here. She is a very charming and beautiful girl, and the most important thing is that she does not seem conscious of her beauty.

I am so glad you were able to get here this week so that we could discuss the things which were bothering you, for I know now you realize just how much you fit into our football plans for the future.

Please remember me to your fine parents and tell your father I am going to be very disappointed if he does not come with you for our picnic on July 30. If your mother would like to come along too, be sure to bring her for my wife, Anne, would be very happy to take care of her.

May I say again that we are very happy to know you will be attending Ohio State this fall.

Your sincere friend,

W. W. Hayes
WWH/g

CHAPTER THREE

OHIO STATE AND WOODY HAYES

LETTER FROM WOODY

The Ohio State University
Department of Physical Education
July 7, 1955

Dear Richard:

I want to get this letter in the mail before my Secretary goes on vacation. It is difficult to realize that within seven weeks from the time you receive this letter, we will be starting Fall practice, and within the following five weeks we will have played two of our nine games. Because of an NCAA rule, we will start practice on Thursday this year rather than on Wednesday. Here are some of the highlights of that five weeks' work.

I am not going to bore you by reminding you that every team we play will be laying for us. You know that just as well as I. There are a few things I would like to mention, however. The first one deals with the fact that we are going to be one of the lightest teams ever to represent Ohio State University. Five of our first six ends weigh a lot less than 200 lbs. each. None of our tackles who started in the Spring game weigh as much as 210. One probable starting guard weighs 188 lbs. And our first four centers will not average 190. Our backfield, with the exception of Vicic, certainly cannot be considered king-size. Don't get the idea, fellows, that I am moaning, because I am not. I feel, although this will be a light team, it will be the fastest football team Ohio State has ever had. We must develop this speed to its absolute maximum. There is only one way to get faster and that is to *run*. By this time your legs should be in good shape. When you work out, if you don't take at least six 30-yard sprints, then you really have not worked out at all.

So often when we think of our National Championship football team, we think of our great offense. It might interest you to know that our offense last year only made a couple more touchdowns than in 1952 and 1953. Then what was the answer? The answer was the great job we did on defense. Just think how much better our tackling was last year. Why was it better? Because of the improvement in our footwork. You can't tackle if your feet can't get you in position *to* tackle. So don't forget to work on those simple little footwork drills which make an agile guy out of you rather than a giant with clay feet. Those drills may look silly, but they certainly pay off.

The third thing I would like to mention is the importance of depth on our team. Last season at six different positions on our team we were forced to start a boy who had been considered a second stringer. In our Michigan game, we lost four boys with injuries in the first half. Two of them never got back in the game. Yet it was a so-called second stringer, Jack Gibbs, who got us back in the ball game with his interception. And it was another so-called second stringer, Fred Kriss, who caught 26 passes in the end zone for our first score. Jerry Hardrader took over and did a terrific job in place of Bob Watkins . . . and Bill Michael and Don Swartz went in and played outstanding ball when we needed them. The reason I mention this is simply the fact that, although you may not be a starter, you very well may be the man to spark us to another National Championship.

The longer I coach, the more I realize that very few athletes ever approach the epitome of their perfection. For this reason, I would like to repeat a paragraph from *Sports Illustrated* of last August 16, which we included in last year's letter to the squad.

It concerns the first two men in the world who broke the four minute mile—Roger Bannister of England and John Landy of Australia.

"Neither Bannister nor Landy has ever been coached. In the casual British club system of competition, unlike the more regimented U.S. college team system, runners are presumed to be able to train themselves. Separately, half a world apart, both Bannister and Landy arrived at curiously identical conclusions; *both decided that over-training and staleness were simply myths and that the more the body endures the more it will endure.* Both drove themselves to extremes of exertion (training sessions of 10 to 14 58-second quarter miles with one lap walked between) which would have staggered the average U.S. athlete."

I cite this paragraph to show what you can do with your body if you really try. I don't expect you to run a four minute mile, but I know, if you push yourself, you can be a greater athlete and bring greater glory to yourself and to Ohio State University than you ever expected. So let's keep punching. If you have not started on your daily training yet, don't put it off till tomorrow—start today.

Your sincere friend,

Woody

Let's hear from you.

GETTING STARTED AT OSU

Baker Hall at Ohio State was my new home. I was not excited about being there. My mind was still on baseball two days before football practice started. I still thought I could make it out of there and join the Cincinnati Reds. If not, I could go into the military. Farming certainly was not in the top ten, but neither was college. I couldn't see four years at Ohio State. Why lose time going to college? But, for the present, I was stuck.

I had played fullback and middle linebacker in high school, but all of a sudden I became a down lineman. Woody gave me three choices—guard, tackle, or end. I chose tackle. I thought it sounded good, and besides, Cy Morgan was a tackle, and Woody had been a tackle at Denison University. It sounded like a challenge and the smart thing to do.

It was a challenge all right. All freshmen were coached by the legendary Ernie Godfrey. (Ironically, he had coached at my hometown college in Wooster before coming to Columbus.) He was an institutional fixture until he died. First day of practice, I was listed tenth string, both right and left tackle. Of course, freshmen could not play varsity ball, so I quickly got lost in the shuffle. I was taking a full load of courses and I had a good job to maintain my scholarship—loading equipment on trucks at a local Ford tractor dealership.

I learned quickly that there was a deep sports tradition at Ohio State. Three revered alumni had been heroes of mine since reading about them as a youngster. One, Chick Harley—All-American. It was said Ohio stadium was built because of him. I was shocked when I got to meet the legend face-to-face when I was a freshman and he came to visit our team. Recently I got to meet many of his relatives and his great-great-great grandson, Robert, who was a senior with the 2004 Buckeyes. Second was Jesse Owens, Olympic gold medalist, from Cleveland, Ohio. Now there's a stadium and track named after him at Ohio State. Third, Paul Brown, the great football coach for Massillon, Ohio State, and the Cleveland Browns, where I later played for him.

ROOMMATES

In 1955 at Ohio State University, freshman football players had to stay on campus in dorms. Maybe they still do. I roomed with several special players: Dick LeBeau, long-time star with the Detroit Lions and, later, defensive coordinator for the Pittsburgh Steelers; Bob White, great All-American fullback who played on the Houston NFL team and later became a school principal; 1958

Sullivan Award-winner Glenn "Jeep" Davis, who, along with Jesse Owens, was the greatest track runner to ever put on the Scarlet and Grey spikes. He was a three-time Olympic gold medalist. Jeep also played two seasons of football with the Detroit Lions. He was born to run and compete. He's still known as the best middle-distance-events runner of all time.

As a senior at Barberton High School, Jeep won the state high school track and field championship by himself with four first-place finishes. At Ohio State, he once won eight events in a dual meet against Penn State, causing the NCAA to limit the number of events one individual can compete in. He won twenty-six Big Ten championships and today is listed among the top one hundred athletes in the world. He ended the incredible streak of 119 consecutive wins in the 120-yard-high hurdles set by Hayes Jones when he beat Jones one on one. Minutes before a race, Jeep would do something that became his trademark. He'd take a few drags from a cigarette. He confided how it relaxed him. His motto was, "There are no excuses. You can win at anything if you work hard enough." Jeep was elected Olympic Torch Bearer in 1996.

Jeep said another thing that I'll never forget: "If you want to be a champion, Schaf, you have to have two messages tattooed on your heart. (1) What I have, I must give it all; (2) Because what I save, I will lose forever."

Jeep stopped by the farm one evening to pick me up for our return to college. I challenged him to a quick game of badminton. We quickly laid out a rough course behind the farmhouse. The winner scores twenty-one points and has to win by two. Jeep beat me two out of three games. For our first two battles, the winner had to score over thirty points. Jeep won the final game 49-47! It was too dark to continue. My two young brothers were the only witnesses to this exciting struggle. I hope to get revenge someday.

A ROCKY START

I didn't have much of a social life on campus. Didn't need one. I drove home most Saturday nights, where I batted stones and helped Dad. I still thought I ought to be playing baseball. During the week I was occupied with football, going to class, and working. Woody gave all players the Royal Canadian Mounted Police exercises to do daily. I did those by the thousands—even in my sleep.

The college classes were mostly lectures. I listened but took no notes and did not study.

I wasn't very happy. After a couple of months, I called the University of Kentucky to find out if they were still interested in having me on the team. No, they weren't. I tried to stay in touch with the Cincinnati Reds. No better reaction. Farming with Dad was looking better each day.

November 1955. On a Sunday night my freshman year, I was ready to leave school for good. I called my parents to tell them I was coming home, but before I could say a word, Mom told me that she, Dad, and close to two hundred of the local townspeople were all coming to watch our practice that next day. It was the Monday before the Michigan game. Uh-oh! What was I to do? I had never practiced against the varsity. I had never even seen the varsity practice. Lord, was I in trouble!

It was about 9:30 p.m. I decided to go directly to Coach Hayes's house and explain this last-minute development. Since Ernie Godfrey was my freshman coach, I had not talked to Woody since football started back in August. The talk was brief. He said, "I'll take care of it. Now go to bed and get a good night's rest." I was nervous as heck not knowing what to expect when the sun came up the next morning. I attended my classes that morning (like that really helped) and reported to practice at 2 p.m. I checked the names on the roster board and, sure enough, on the "Dog Meat" freshman group was my name. I was to line up in a maize and blue jersey on the defense across from Jim Parker, an All-American guard, at six foot three and 265 pounds. Beside "Big Jim" and playing tackle was six foot four, 275-pound guard Bill Cummings. I was six foot three and 215 pounds.

As we all trotted onto the practice field, I noticed Mom and Dad with all their friends gathered at one end of the field. They recognized me right away and were waving even though I had no number on my jersey. Nobody lower than the eighth team had a number, but they were cheering me anyway. God, was that embarrassing! Practice began. First play straight at me. Second, third, and fourth play straight at me.

Woody was bent over, hands on his knees, before each play. He'd pull his cap on real tight like it was going to fly away and would stare at me. He was getting more and more emotional and yelling louder with each play. He was staring at me like he was saying, have you had enough? Do you want to quit? Feel sorry for yourself?

Before each play, I could see a twinkle in Parker's and Cummings's eyes as they were coming to the line of scrimmage. Parker would say, "Coming at you again, Schaf-tee." A few times, to add insult to injury, he added the starting-count number, too.

At one time during that practice, Woody ran ten straight plays at me. I recalled what he had had said the night before: "Better get a good night's rest!" I was starting to breathe harder and harder. Each play I fought to stay on my feet for at least a second before I was crushed under the weight of Parker and Cummings. They double-teamed me, sometimes as far as ten yards down the field before I was laid to rest. As practice ended, there was grass and mud stuck all over my helmet, my neck, and down my pants. I was bleeding from the nose and mouth. I had a black eye, bruised ribs, and a broken finger, and muscle spasms started popping out from head to toe.

My mom and dad were so pleased to see that I was in the middle of all the action. Afterwards they and their friends took me to a local White Castle restaurant. I looked like a beat-up, sad-faced hound dog. I hardly ate a bite. Everybody was jabbering and slapping me on the back with good intentions. I was never so sore and whipped in my life. I was limping, bleeding, and picking dirt out of my teeth, ears, and fingernails weeks later!

I batted a lot of stones into the barnyard after fall quarter. I had failed two courses, but I decided things couldn't get much worse so I agreed to go back for winter quarter and try again. Woody and Anne Hayes decided I should stay some at their home and study, especially on weekends. I lived there off and on for the next year and a half. Every time I'd wanted to leave school, he'd barricade me in his house.

THE OSU FOOTBALL PROGRAM

During 1955, it seemed someone within the Buckeye inner circle was jealous of Woody's quick success. He couldn't really be this good. A suspicious writer from *Sports Illustrated* magazine arrived on campus and stayed for several months. Everything went ahead pretty much as normal until, POW! An article in early 1956 hits the paper. "The Ohio State University Football program was like the football tail wagging the University Dog." The writer was supported in his remarks by Ohio State Alumni Association secretary Jack Fullen. It was later rumored that Mr. Fullen was trying to get his name out there to become the university's next athletic director. Woody was convinced Fullen influenced the Ohio State faculty to vote against the Buckeyes representing the Big Ten in the 1961 Rose Bowl. Mr. Fullen became a constant pain in the neck for Woody and the players until he left in the mid-'60s.

Some people criticized Buckeye football because Coach Hayes and his wife entertained, housed, and fed some players. They gave financial assistance to players in need and passed out loans and gifts all over the place. Anne treated the players like family. A full-time tutor had also become available to players; Woody even had the gall to stay night and day in a dorm with his players during training camp. This close relationship was out of the ordinary. If not stopped, it could get out of control in a hurry.

Woody admitted to some of these things. He did help some players in need by giving small loans, and most of the players paid him back. However, he said he never gave luxury gifts. He could not produce any records of these transactions as there was nothing in writing. Woody said he did not know his actions were in violation of NCAA rules. As a result, all Ohio State sports programs were put on probation for the 1956 season. Even if eligible, the football team could not go to the Rose Bowl.

The following year, the NCAA changed a few specific rules for scholarship athletes. They must maintain a 1.8 grade-point average. The football program could help all athletes with financial needs whether they qualified as needy or not. And tutors were now allowed.

Then, suddenly, a lot of meaningless jobs appeared. They were created to help those most in need. A requirement was you had to sign in and out to get paid.

Spring quarter, 1956. I reported to the Ohio Stadium with a teammate three evenings a week. We'd flip a coin to see who would turn the stadium lights on or off. Sometimes we'd keep the lights going on and off all night. Just kidding—there were no lights. Other players had jobs like making sure stadium walls had no cracks, keeping tornado watch, and making sure fire extinguishers were hanging. One guy told me he was in charge of maintenance for forty years and wrote checks to players that never worked a day. They just signed in and out. Some players needed money to survive. Everyone needed change for the phone, clothes, extra food, laundry, gasoline for the car, books, etc.

From 1955 to 1958, freshmen could not play varsity ball. Each Big Ten football team played only nine games. And if you were fortunate enough to play in the Rose Bowl game, you could not do it again the next year. Every player had to stay on the field for all offense, defense, and special teams. If you came out of the game for any reason, you could not go back until the next quarter. The night before a game, all players attended the same movie together, one that Woody felt was G-rated. All players had to be in their room with lights out by 11 p.m. All players ate four hours before the game. No players or coaches were allowed to wear gloves during practice or games. All players had to wear a shirt and tie to and from games. The team said a prayer together before going on the field prior to start of each game. Everybody wore single-bar face masks, but no mouth guards were required. As an added note, no blacks had been allowed on the team until the early 1940s. Before the 1950s a player couldn't have an athletic scholarship if married.

My official roommate Winter Quarter 1956 was our outstanding Halfback, Dick LeBeau. But Dick and I didn't see much of each other off the field. Nobody saw much of me. I made up two failed courses, carried a full load again, continued working the same two jobs, one full-time, the other part-time, and stayed at Woody's house a couple days a week.

During spring quarter I was back in good academic standing, but I was getting itchy to play baseball. I went out for the baseball team. Why not? Galen Cisco, our fullback, did. I was really excited about the possibilities. Of course, Woody found out two days later and nixed everything. I was back out for spring football practices and listed as the same tenth-string tackle. I failed a course again and was ineligible for football the next fall season.

I was ready to head south for summer baseball. The Reds still sounded like they might be interested, but first my parents said I had to have another talk with Coach Hayes. By now Woody had me registered for summer school to make up the failed course and, for good measure, added an additional one, his "Football 101" class. It was to be taught by his offensive tackle coach, Bill Hess. How convenient!

Enter summer school. With Anne my as own daily tutor, how could I not do well? I played handball against Woody every morning, did Royal Canadian push-ups and pull-ups by the thousands. A fellow teammate, Tom Baldacci, took the football class with me under Coach Hess. We were the only two who had to be fully dressed in our football uniforms because Coach Hess used us as demonstrators. He was a stickler on fundamentals. Head up! Eyes on the target! Never cross your feet! Shoulder explosion! Head priority! Keep butt down! I was driving the blocking sled and actually starting to like it. I finished summer school and got As in both the make-up class and Football 101. Now I was eligible for varsity football!

I liked being pushed, challenged, and competing at anything. And Woody knew how to fire me up! I'd run through walls for the guy. I loved the emotional part of Woody—that was the ultimate! He gave the sport all he had and more. He was born with a fiery spirit and was obsessed with winning. He loved Ohio State—the team, the fans, the whole state. Watching him ripping his hat apart, throwing his watch against a wall, jumping on his glasses, kicking yard markers—who could ask for more? During my career, he also had great assistants—Bill Hess, Lyle Clark, Ernie Godfrey, Esco Sarkkinen, Harry Stroebel, Bo Schembechler, Gene Fekete, and others.

And then there was John Bozick, the Ohio State equipment manager. Boz is something special. The most loyal and respected guy I know. A legend. The superintendent of jocks and socks. He deserves to be in the Ohio State Hall of Fame. He's already forgotten more happenings than most former athletes remember. Several years ago, the Alumni Association's Board of Directors awarded Boz with an Honorary Varsity "O".

SOPHOMORE YEAR

When football started in the fall of 1956, I was in great shape at 215 pounds. I was shocked to see that Coach Hayes had moved me up to fourth on the depth charts at both left and right tackle before the first practice. My football number was picked as 71, but the possibility of playing in a game was not too good. Substitutes did not play unless there was an injury. Starters played nearly all sixty minutes. There were no specialists

The start of the second week of practice, I was moved to third-string tackle, left and right. Then the second stringer left tackle twisted his ankle. Everything was happening really fast! I did not have time to reflect on anything. Fall quarter classes were about to start, and we were getting ready for our first game. Now I was on the brink of playing as first replacement on either side. Coming out of the tunnel for that first game, my feet never touched the ground! I got into the game for two series towards the end of the fourth quarter.

That year we played against some really good quarterbacks. Don Meredith, SMU, later, Dallas Cowboys; John Brodie, Stanford, later, the 49ers; Lenny Dawson, Purdue, later, the Browns and Chiefs, and Milt Plum, Penn State, later, the Browns and Lions. In 1955, the team had played against Duke's great All-American, Sonny

Jurgeson, who played with the Redskins. The second game I was sent in during the second quarter and tackled Don Meredith for a 10-yard loss. I remembered at that moment what my friend and former high school history teacher Don Welch said: "If and when you get your chance, try to make something big happen!" The next two games I played about 50 percent of the time. All of a sudden, I became the starting left tackle right alongside All-American guard Jim Parker. "Big Jim" was great at standing his man straight up. I'd block down, and together we'd give the defender a good ride. Boy, was that fun! I was still recalling the year before when one Monday afternoon Big Jim and Bill Cummings were having fun rolling me around.

The highlight of my first regular season was winning our seventeenth straight Big Ten game. But then, the following week, we lost 6-0 to Iowa. Woody went crazy after the game! He was chasing the news media out of the dressing room, breaking cameras, and kicking and punching those not leaving fast enough.

Toughest game I played in that season was against Michigan. My opponent was Ron Kramer, an All-American offensive end. He was a great blocker and used me as his personal blocking sled. He turned me inside-out most of the first half. But I got better and blocked one of his field goal attempts during the second half. I remember Bobby Mitchell, the great halfback from Illinois. He was the quickest guy I ever saw. He averaged nearly twenty yards a carry against us, but he fumbled a couple of times and we outscored them. Later he was my teammate with the Cleveland Browns. I also remember playing opposite Paul Wiggin, an All-American end from Stanford who later became a teammate with the Browns. And another future Browns teammate, Jim Shofner, All-American running back from Texas Christian University.

With the Buckeyes, we would throw the ball maybe only three or four times a game. In 1956, our halfback, Don Clark, was leading passer in total yards for the season—6 for 88 yards. On all short yardage or goal line plays, Woody referred to every run from tackle to tackle as "Patton plays" (after General Patton). It was as if we didn't make the first down or touchdown, we'd lose the war.

The night before all games in our bedrooms, there would be a pint of cold milk, a cookie, and an apple for each player. Woody didn't expect you to be hungry on game day.

I LAND ON MY FEET

In 1957, during the spring quarter of my junior year, I wanted to go out for baseball again. Of course, Woody nixed the idea immediately. I worked hard and received a trophy after spring practice as the most improved player. He told me if I kept the same attitude and commitment, I could possibly become an All-American. I went home to work that summer. I helped on the farm, had a construction job, and played on three baseball teams. I really had fun!

We started fall football practice with one goal—the Rose Bowl. I was in great shape! I could do seventy-five push-ups on my fingertips in one minute flat. I could do forty pull-ups, the standard way with your hands towards your body, then immediately reverse the hands and do forty more. Jim Marshall, who later played nineteen years with the Minnesota Vikings, and I were the only ones who could challenge each other.

Woody had told everybody before reporting to fall practice to have their hair cut short. Dick LeBeau had a large female fan club and to please them, he had grown Jimmy Dean's hairstyle of long locks and sideburns. Woody was not impressed. He said after our first workout that Dick had to get to a barber. I said, "Hey, Coach, my dad cuts hair and I know how to do it. Besides, it would be free." Ten minutes later, LeBeau was in the chair with a sheet around his shoulders.

It was a hot day and I was really sweating. I gave Dick a towel to keep wiping my face so I could see better. He kept saying, "Are you okay, Schaf? Schaf, you've never cut hair before, have you? Tell me the truth, Schaf." I said, "Well, kind of. I've sheared a few sheep." He said, "I thought so! Hurry up and finish the job. Just quit pretending and messing around." He was more than a little upset. "Cut it all off! It looks like heck the way it is." So, I shaved him bald, Dad's style! It only took a couple more minutes. LeBeau didn't need a comb for a couple of months. Woody loved it! No one else ever volunteered for me to cut their hair. It was my first and last haircut.

After practice Woody put us both on his weekly TV show. He wanted to showcase our hair-cutting ordeal. Dick was still looking grumpy. Woody recognized LeBeau as a good student, football player, and talented singer and dancer. He also noted that his teammates had persuaded him to have his locks trimmed. It would be a good example to Ohio's youth. Lastly, he praised me for volunteering to be his barber. Fifty years later, LeBeau still remembers that event.

Every coach I've ever played for liked to use one player as an example to try and motivate his teammates. For the 1957 and 1958 Buckeyes, that player was Dick LeBeau. Without fail, every Monday Woody would post his first, second, and third team. Dick was always on the third team. He could gain three-hundred yards and score six touchdowns, and he was third team. Game day, LeBeau was starting halfback.

We'd all pull his string and razz him everyday during practices. He didn't like it, but accepted his role.

It was our year, 1957. We won the Big Ten, went to the Rose Bowl, beat Oregon, and were national champions. I averaged fifty-eight minutes a game playing both ways. The key to that season was the Iowa game. The Hawkeyes had upset us the previous year and many of their players were back, including Alex Karras, an All-American, a huge defensive tackle who went on to play for the Detroit Lions for twelve years. The game was in Ohio Stadium so we had our home crowd behind us. Still, we were behind by four points with three minutes to go, and there was more than seventy yards between us and pay dirt. It was a typical Hayes drive—every play between their tackles with LeBeau and White running straight at Karras and their other tackle, Kline.

Bob White was a one-man wrecking crew. The best two-way college player I ever saw. He excelled at three positions: fullback, guard, and linebacker. He was also a good kicker at punting and kickoffs. Bob was a legitimate All-American.

To offset the physical capabilities of Karras and Kline, our line

had to get into their minds a bit. Our offensive tackles always called
the line-blocking assignments at the line of scrimmage. When we
called "Rack it," our tight end and tackle double-teamed the defensive tackle. Jim Houston and I were double-teaming Klein, and
we rode him out of there three times in a row. So when we get in
the huddle the next time, Jim says, "Hey, Schaf! Call 'rack it' when
you're gonna double-team with the guard and let's see what Klein
does." I get to the line and call "Rack it!" and Klein thinks Jim and I
are coming at him again. He dives outside at Houston and falls flat
on his face. I'm double-teaming inside with my guard, Jobco, and
a hole opens up and White goes for about ten! White carried the
ball almost every play. We gave the ball to LeBeau once or twice,
but we only netted a couple of yards. Woody said, "The hell with
that! Keep giving the ball to White!" So it went all the way to victory. Many times in practice we'd come to the line and point at
someone and say, "We're coming over you" and the player didn't
know whether to believe us or not. It was great when it worked a
couple times in this game. Iowa couldn't stop us, and we scored.
Vice-President Richard Nixon was in the stands and later came to
our dressing room to celebrate with us as Woody's guest.

After the game, LeBeau and I were walking back to my apartment. As we started across the stadium parking lot, I collapsed
when muscle spasms started knotting up my whole body from not
drinking enough water. Dick tried to help but couldn't. He raced
back to the dressing room and brought the trainer with him. Boy,
was that painful.

I got clipped from behind just before halftime against Michigan
and hurt my knee. We won the game and I got my Michigan gold
pants. The trainers didn't think I could recover in time to play in
the Rose Bowl game, but I did.

A ROSE BOWL HONEYMOON

Bonnie Flickinger, my girlfriend since high school, and I decided to get married early and treat the Rose Bowl trip as our honeymoon. It was not very romantic. Woody never let us stay together

in California. She was working full time as secretary for the dean of the College of Agriculture at OSU. We had the wedding ceremony the first week in December, and I was granted a wheelchair to sit on because of my bum knee. My grandfather loved watching Bonnie constantly standing and kneeling during the Catholic ceremony while I just sat there. I could hear him snickering throughout the entire proceedings.

NATIONAL CHAMPIONS

The day the team was to leave for California, I was driving alone down old State Route 3 from Wooster to Columbus. About thirty miles north of Columbus, I was pulled over for speeding. I pleaded with the officer to be lenient since we were going to leave for the Rose Bowl in two hours. The officer handed me a warning and wished me good luck. About two hours later, three of my teammates, Bill Wentz, Al Crawford, and Jim Houston, were traveling the same road to Columbus, and they got stopped by the same officer. Wouldn't you know they used the same line! The officer said, "You know, boys, I stopped one of your teammates, Dick Schafrath, about two hours ago, and he said the plane would be leaving in about two hours. If that's true, you guys already missed your flight. I'm giving you a warning. Take it easy and beat Oregon!"

Our friends at Wooster decided to help Mom and Dad go to the Rose Bowl, too. They raised enough money to give them a round-trip plane ride and ten days at a beautiful hotel in Pasadena. It was like a script from *The Beverly Hillbillies*. Dad tried to get on the plane out of Columbus with a bucket of dirt so he could keep his "feet on the ground." The pilot let him sit in the co-pilot seat during most of the flight. Mom and Dad attended all the Rose Bowl events as well as a day at Disneyland. At one party Dad and teammate Ron Cook both got to dance a few seconds with an actress named Jayne Mansfield. They also met many other stars like John Wayne, Doris Day, Bob Hope, and Jimmy Stewart. Their favorite attraction was the Rose Bowl parade. They, along with Bonnie, had a great time together. All I can remember about that game was the hype all week. My memories instead include going to Disneyland and Sea World, attending several dinners with our opponents from Oregon, and seeing movie stars and the Rose Bowl floats.

It was hard to practice and stay focused—none of us had been to the West Coast before. It was exciting to play in front of 100,000 people. We were favored to win by 19 points. The final was a close 10-7, Buckeyes victory. Both teams played their hearts out. Don Sutherlin, our great field goal kicker, was the difference. One writer later wrote, "Never did a team with so much do so little and a team with so little do so much." Yeah! What matters is we won and were National Champions. Number two for Woody and his Buckeyes.

SENIOR YEAR, 1958

In 1958, my senior year, I was elected co-captain of the team with Frank Kremblan, our quarterback from Akron St. Vincent. We knew we could not go to the Rose Bowl again or play in any other bowl, but we still had a good season with some excellent players. I was returning with 473 playing-time minutes for ten games in 1957. We beat Michigan and I got my second gold pants. Over my three varsity seasons, sixteen teammates were drafted and went on to play professional football: Frank Kremblan (QB), New York Giants; Jim Houston (LB), Cleveland; Dick LeBeau (HB), Detroit Lions; Tom Matte (HB), Baltimore Colts; Jim Marshall, (Tackle) Minnesota Vikings; Jim Tyer (Tackle), Kansas City Chiefs; Al Crawford (Tackle), New York Titans; Dan James (Center) and John Scott (Tackle), Pittsburgh Steelers; Ernie Wright (Tackle) and Bob White (FB), Houston Oilers; Aurelius Thomas (Guard), Canada; and Bill Jobko (Guard), Atlanta. Frank Machinsky, Don Clark, and Don Sutherin all went to Canada. Jim Parker and Howard Cassady had left earlier to play pro ball with the Colts and Lions. Lenny Fontes later became assistant coach with the Detroit Lions.

I was a 1958 pre-season All-American pick at tackle. One week before the first game, our regular starting end, Rusty Bowermaster, broke his ankle. Woody came to me that night, woke me up out of a sleep, and said, "Dick, the coaches and I keep counting our best eleven players to have on the field at the same time. Three of them are always tackles—Marshall, Tyer, and yourself. What do you think we should do?" I answered without hesitation, "It's me, Coach." His next words were, "Why don't you sleep on this before you make a final decision?" I walked down the hall to end coach Esco Sarkkinen's room and spent half the night going over end assignments with him. Woody at one time prepared me to split out as a lonesome end for a whole game because he saw Army make a big play doing that. I was out there for a quarter or so and then I said to myself, "To heck with this." Woody never tried throwing me the ball even though no one tried to cover me, so I went back to tight end. I caught probably six or seven passes the whole year, one for forty-five yards and a touchdown.

Until Woody died he always said two things about me: I gave up being a possible All-American to help the team, and I did not get my college degree despite his promise to my parents. I learned a lot of good fundamentals when I switched to playing end, and I'm confident it helped me to be a better pro-football player. Many times the All-American tag is blown out of proportion. A lot of successful professional athletes were not All-Americans. They were great team players that had a passion to win. Woody likened it to the idea that many successful businessmen are not the ones with the most talent and degrees, trophies and ribbons. Woody was always telling people that I was his best conditioned athlete and best down-field blocker he ever coached. We finished the season with one loss and were ranked sixth in the nation.

I was named Lineman of the Week against the Badgers and Co-Lineman against Purdue. I finished the season as Player of the Game against Michigan.

AN IMPORTANT FINISH

We were leading Michigan 20-14. It was the last minute of the game. They were on our 3rd-yard line—first and goal, a minute to go. Wolverine halfback Brad Meyers took a handoff and was headed in my direction. I slipped my blocker and popped him hard in midsection. I knew I had stopped him for no gain. He fumbled the ball. We recovered and the Buckeyes had our gold pants!

A LOT HAPPENED DURING MY TIME AT OHIO STATE
(1955–1958, AND INCLUDING 1954)

Established new record—17 conference wins consecutively
Big Ten champions three times (1954, 1955, 1957)
Rose Bowl champions twice
National champions twice
Beat Michigan four times! (1954, 1955, 1957, 1958)
We passed the football less each year, thus the title, "three yards and a cloud of dust"
Our opponent's defenses tried 6-, 7-, 8-, and 9-man fronts against us
One Heisman Trophy winner
Played 9-game seasons
One year probation (1956)

WOODY HAYES

Woody was my friend, coach, mentor, and hero for thirty-three years, from 1954 until his death in 1987. He was the biggest "giving" person in the United States. He stayed close to players and their families, visited hospitals and sick people across the state, yet kept his own health problems to himself. Each year he would visit visited war-torn areas, especially Vietnam. He was a close friend of President Nixon and General Westmoreland.

For fifteen to twenty years of Woody's life, he was diabetic. He never wanted anyone to know, and he never used the disease as a crutch. But I knew, and several people close to him knew. We all honored his request to keep the diabetes a secret. It explains a lot of his unusual behavior the last few years of his life. He'd meet his doctors in private places at unusual hours. If he were still alive, he'd be kicking my butt big time for even mentioning this.

Money was no goal of Woody's. When he died his wife Anne and son Steve found piles of envelopes with uncashed checks and cash in his office desk and home dresser. Thousands of dollars—untouched! His life was all about work, people, relationships, winning, and paying forward.

WOODY STORIES

In the locker room before football games, Woody would get very emotional and excited. Lots of "dag gummits, well hells, damns, and g. damns." One time, he put his fist through a blackboard that was sitting on the easel. He could not get his arm back out. Two players grabbed hold of the board while Woody jumped around trying to kick it off. He finally shook his arm loose. Some years later, I asked Anne about his irate actions, and she told me how Woody was constantly sending her to the store to purchase "cheap items" so he could use them in pre-game talks. Woody would hire officials to officiate our practices, then chase them off the field if they called a penalty or, better yet, if they wouldn't call a penalty! They couldn't win no matter how hard they tried. He hated striped shirts!

During practices or games in the 1950s and early '60s, no matter what the temperature or weather, Woody never wore a long-sleeved shirt, jacket, or gloves. He maintained it was all in your head. If you didn't think about it, it wouldn't bother you. He had all coaches get their pockets—whether in their shirts, pants, or coats, sewn shut. Finally, on the advice of trainers and doctors, he started wearing long-sleeved shirts and jackets. But never wore stocking caps or gloves.

At the heat of a moment, Woody would fire his coaches. If you weren't fired five or six times a season, you weren't doing your job. He'd forget about it fifteen minutes later.

When traveling, whatever bus Woody was in, all players tried to get into the other bus.

One time Woody was upset at the team for a loss. He said, "It's the coaches' fault. We're not working hard enough!" He had the players all sit in the grass in the stadium field to watch the coaches.

He said, "Come on men. It starts with us. We have to set a better example for our team. We're going to run the stadium steps." They all looked at him stunned. They started jogging, got halfway up the first deck, slowed to a walk, then most stopped and sat down. He said, "Oh hell, we proved a point! Let's go back and practice."

When he was once asked why he went for two points against Michigan with the game about over and a thirty-point lead he responded, "We couldn't go for three."

Woody remained persistent and stubborn as heck. I remember one time being at his office and watching him trying to park his car. He had his same parking space next to the Armory at St. John's Arena for years. This day, there were two cars parked over the lines, squeezing both sides of his space. Woody slowly pulled in between them, tried to get out the door, then tried to crawl out the window but couldn't. I thought he finally had given up. He backed out of the space, got out of his car, shut the door, got behind it, and pushed it back into the parking space, put a stone behind the tire, and walked into his office like nothing happened.

TY SCHAFRATH AND WOODY

One of my sons, Ty, attended college for two and one-half years at Ohio Wesleyan. He left school for a year and worked for Disney-World in Florida. He decided he wanted to be an artist, and his school was going to be the art college at Ohio State! It was late May and he was excited as heck as we both drove to Columbus. After standing in the registration line for an hour or so, it was finally his turn. Ty said to the woman in charge, "Hi, my name's Ty Schafrath and I'd like to enroll for fall quarter. Here are my transcripts from Ohio Wesleyan." We were greeted with loud, gut-wrenching laughter. "Who do you think you are? President Reagan? You're about three months too late! If you apply now you'll be lucky to get into winter quarter. Personally, I'd recommend your best bet is to go back to OW. Okay, next person."

I kept my mouth shut—I don't know why. I guess I was taken aback by this humbling and embarrassing experience. I can still see the clerk motioning her hand for us to get out of her way. We left with our heads between our legs. We walked around the campus for awhile until I finally said, "Hey Ty, let's stop by and see Coach Hayes before we leave." During our visit, Coach said, "Ty, why aren't you going to Ohio State where your dad attended?" We told him the registration-desk story. Woody immediately called the dean of the art college, then told us to hurry over and see him. We were escorted right into the dean's office where we had a great five-minute talk. He left the room for a couple of minutes, then returned and told Ty to go back to the same registration desk. We thanked him and said good-bye.

After leaving, we looked at each other and said, "This will be interesting." We were told to go immediately to the head of the line. Yep, the same woman. The proper papers were ready, her attitude had changed, and she wished us well. Ty was in for fall quarter thanks to the dean and Coach Hayes!

NURSE WOODY

In July 1985, I was told I needed to have a medical procedure, and in my case "delicate" was the appropriate term. I had to undergo a hemorrhoid operation which, of course, I was not too thrilled about. As the appointed day approached, I was very apprehensive and soon became quite depressed.

At the time I was between marriages, and my kids were hither and yon, so I decided to ask my friend Patrick Leahy if he'd go with me. He said, "Sure, Schaf—no problem." On the way to the hospital I told Patrick to call Anne Hayes and tell her I was in the hospital. I hoped Woody would stop by during my convalescence.

The "medical procedure" was about to take place. After my spinal block, I was placed in a very strange position, as you might imagine, so the doctor could have an excellent view of the working area. Since I was awake I started to tell the doctors and attending folks alike football stories, which, of course, included Woody.

Following the operation, I was put in a post-op room for a short period of time and then returned to my room. Standing there was

Patrick with a smirk on his face. I wondered if he was happy to see me alive or surprised I hadn't died from apprehension. Neither was true. I asked him why the smile. He said that after the operation was over, the anesthetist came to tell him I had survived—but he was almost inaudible because he was bent over in laughter. Patrick, who had heard all of my stories many times given our long association, asked me if I was nuts giving my choice of entertainment in the doctor's positioning. Well, it proves my theory that giggles are important to good health.

It was getting to be early evening when we heard the hall begin to echo with the words, "Hi, Coach Woody, nice to see you again, Woody," and a chorus of similar greetings. The "Big Fellow" was on the floor and coming to see me. My spirits were immediate buoyed. He was a legend at all of the hospitals in Columbus because he constantly visited patients young and old. He was unquestionably the best-known visitor at hospitals all over the state.

Woody entered and said, "Well, Richard, how are you doing?" He always called me Richard, and I was really happy to see my coach and friend. For the next two hours he told us stories and gave his opinion on various topics. During our session with him I mentioned, "You know, Coach, you should still be coaching." He said, "No, I really should have retired a year earlier than I did." He was a great man, and it was just a pleasure to be with him.

Even though we had a long visit and we were all tired from a long day, I was sorry he was leaving. I told him to say hi to Anne, and he was out the door. The chorus of greetings returned from the employees as he left the hospital and disappeared into the night.

WOODY'S SAYINGS

We always expect to win.
We win with people.
Fumbles are caused because of carelessness.
The passing game is like a plague.
I will never alibi—when it's over it's over.
Stick to what you believe is right, even if you're wrong.

Don't give me any pity. Team mistakes are mine.

I sometimes lose because I make dumb mistakes.

I'd like to swing at the face in the mirror.

When you're winning you don't need friends—when you lose you don't need friends either.

Like I said, we're going to get in two hours of work even if it takes us six.

Most people change early, but when people change too late you have a problem. Like the problem we had in high school. They had to give up driver's ed because the horse died.

You don't get hurt running straight ahead three yards and a cloud of dust—I will pound you and pound you until you give up.

I love football and I despise losing.

Anything that comes easy is not worth a damn.

Without winners there would be no civilization.

Statistics always reminds me of the fellow who drowned in a river three-feet deep.

I'm not trying to win a popularity contest; I'm trying to win football games.

There's nothing that cleanses your soul like getting the hell kicked out of you.

And then, in 1955, after a Rose Bowl win: "They weren't that good. I know four other Big Ten teams that could have beaten them."

Woody always quoted General George Patton: Our basic game plan is to advance and keep advancing regardless of the elements—and we will go over, under, and through the enemy until we reach our destination.

PRO FOOTBALL

CHAPTER FOUR

THE CLEVELAND BROWNS

DRAFTED

I was drafted into the NFL on the Monday after OSU's last game against Michigan. I was the third of eight Buckeye players to be drafted from that great Buckeye team in 1958. The Browns chose me behind Rich Kreitling, an end from the University of Illinois. The gentleman in charge of the Browns' draft choices was talent scout Dick Gallagher, an old friend of Hank Critchfield's. Dick LeBeau was the Browns' next pick.

I was out of town on a short vacation and didn't even know that the draft was being held. I learned the results four days later. The atmosphere then was quite different from what it is today. Now the NFL draft hyped for at least a week ahead of time and then televised nationwide. Of course, today a player's position in the draft means a lot of money. The difference being drafted then and now means millions of dollars. Money was not our incentive in the 1950s. My first salary was $600 a month, and I was glad to get it. I couldn't believe they were willing to pay me anything to play for a team that I loved so much. But all players and coaches in pro ball played for the challenge and fun of it. They had off-season jobs to survive.

I often joke that I had to take a cut in pay to leave Ohio State. The truth is, I never even asked how much money I would make with the Browns. Paul Brown sent me a contract, and I signed it and sent it back. I think my contract also called for a $750 signing bonus to purchase a car. There were some rumors that Paul took the bonus back if you made the team; if you got cut, you got to keep it. In any event, I made the team and he let me keep the bonus.

GOOD-BYE, COLLEGE DIPLOMA

I got picked for a few all-star bowl games at the end of the college season. That December and January I played in the Blue-Gray, North-South, and the Senior Bowl games. When I accepted $500 for playing in the Senior Bowl, I lost my scholarship at Ohio State. I didn't learn that I had lost it until two weeks into the quarter. I used the money to pay off some loans and a few other expenses and left school. I never took time to cancel my courses; I just left. So I received sixteen hours of failing grades.

Good-bye, college diploma.

Like Mark Twain said, "I never let my schooling get in the way of my education." I went back to Wooster and started working for a construction company to stay in shape, make a little money, and prepare for the Browns' training camp. I also joined the U.S. Air Force Reserves and spent two months in basic training at Lackland Air Force Training Base.

That summer I was one of six players selected to represent the Browns. We were to play for the College All-Stars in their annual summer game in Chicago against the defending NFL champions, the Colts. It was the Baltimore Colts who had defeated the New York Giants the previous December in what many people describe as "The Greatest Football Game Ever Played." You can imagine how excited we were to be going up against them.

THE COLLEGE ALL-STAR GAME, 1959

Upon arrival in Chicago, all the college all-stars were handed rule sheets for the week by Coach Otto Graham. We were to practice two weeks on the campus of Northwestern University, then play the game at historic Soldier's Field.

After looking over the rules and expectations of Coach Graham, I didn't double-check curfew time. I thought it said 11 p.m. What it really said was: In your rooms at 10:30 p.m., lights out at 11 p.m.

The first night I came into the hotel lobby at 10:45 and got a milk-shake in the coffee shop where the coaches were all seated. I waved at them, they waved back, and I went to my room.

The next day, after a long, hot, hard practice, Coach Graham called the names of three guys to stick around and do extra drills for missing curfew. Wooten, O'Brien, and Schafrath. All Browns. He made us all leapfrog for 100 yards, then turn around and log-roll over one another, then run like a bear on all fours for the next 100 yards, and then sprint 100 yards. Then we had to do 'em over again until we got sick.

The same three guys had their names called the next day. We were on our backs gasping for air, and Wooten says, "Schaf, what time is curfew?" I said, "I think eleven o'clock." John said, "I thought so, too. Let's check this thing out." Needless to say, we didn't miss curfew again.

In Chicago, I had a pretty good game going. I was alternating playing guard and center because of a few injuries we had on our line. At 220 pounds, I was sometimes playing across from Big Daddy Lipscomb, who weighed close to 300 pounds. Boy, was he big and fast! He could pick two or three of us up at one time and sort us out until he found the ball carrier. At the beginning of the third quarter, while protecting our punter, I got hit by an elbow in the face, which cracked my cheekbone near the eye socket. I also had a head concussion, so off I went to the hospital for a night of rest. Four of my teammates were also hospitalized.

The next morning I checked myself out of the hospital at 8 a.m. and decided to drive to the Browns training camp in Hiram. I called and said, "I'm on my way. I'll be there soon." I got confused and drove the wrong direction. A couple of hours later I called the camp again. I said, "I'm almost in St. Louis. I'm changing directions and coming back." When I arrived at the Ohio line, Paul Brown had a Highway Patrol car waiting for me, and they drove me the rest of the way to Hiram. I rested for a week before the doctors said it was okay to start practice.

PAUL BROWN'S TEST

I passed Paul Brown's mental test. Paul had exceptionally high standards for his players. Each year, on opening day of camp at Hiram College, everyone had to take an IQ test. It was a tough four-hour military-type test. Flunk it and you had a bus ticket home the next morning. No plane tickets in those days.

Paul would never reveal your grade. He did confide in those close to him that Frank Ryan, with an IQ of 156, scored the highest in Browns history followed by Chuck Noll and Paul Wiggin.

Paul used it in many ways to check the learning capabilities of his players and their character. This helped to alert him on how to teach and prevent problems. He wanted to treat all players the same, and he felt the test was a useful tool for doing just that. He also placed great emphasis on character, behavior, class, and intelligence—all necessary championship ingredients. His test today would be called a "psychological" or "personality" test.

Today the players' union does not permit testing of veteran players—only free agents and rookies. Before they sign a contract, they are asked to take the test.

A player must be given results of the test if he wants to know.

According to Paul's son, Mike Brown, the idea for the test came from what the armed services administered during both WWI and WWII. Personally, I never knew or cared to know my results. I'd be surprised if I was more than average.

The next test was my physical. It was very basic, and I passed. However, a potential problem loomed for me with the weigh-in. Paul wanted his tackles to weigh at least 240 pounds and I was only about 220. I had the answer: For the weigh-in, I had the construction company I worked for in Wooster make me a twenty-five-pound iron jock strap. It was held up by suspenders under my T-shirt. Paul Brown was looking at the scales and couldn't believe his eyes. The scales said I weighed 252! He said, "My goodness, you don't look that heavy, Schaf. Get back on the scales." Then he discovered the iron jock. He said, "Schafrath, anybody that would go to those extremes to weigh 250 pounds, I'm going to give you a chance to play. Just make sure you gain twenty-five to thirty pounds by the end of the season." I did gain the weight and more.

I was the first guy on the Browns to lift weights, but Paul Brown didn't believe in weights. He liked his players lean. No NFL coach asked you to lift weights. They thought it would make you too tight and muscle-bound. That was before 1960. I visited a boxing gym where Jimmy Bivins, a great old-time Hall of Fame boxer, trained in Cleveland. They worked with me on how to lift weights properly, and I gained that fifty pounds in six months. Because of my experience with them, I built my own gym in my garage. Dad helped me build barbells out of tractor axles and other farm equipment.

PAUL BROWN'S RULES OF FAIR PLAY

At the beginning of camp, Paul Brown handed out notebooks to each player and made us write down every assignment for every player and every play. He insisted we commit to memory a lot of pigskin platitudes. Example: The punt is the only play in football that continually gains fifty yards. Paul said his goal was to prove that the same ideas that won for him in high school and college could win in the pros.

Paul always had rules. In high school, you could not date during the football season. In college and Browns training camp, and on pre-game night, lights out at 11 p.m. And he had fines for everything. Late to practice, late to meetings, late for bed check, smoking, or drinking in public. Having sex after Tuesday, but I'm not sure that he ever enforced that one! But he made sure that every wife knew about the rule. Also, there was a fine for not giving your best effort or for making a mental mistake.

WHO WAS COACH BROWN?

Paul Brown was unique. He easily could have been president of General Motors or Harvard. He was a genius at organization. He introduced the word "organization" and taught it to the NFL. His life was about football even from his early years, when the Massillon Pro Tigers football team featuring Knute Rockne, was always battling cross town rival Canton Pro Bulldogs and Jim Thorpe.

Paul played quarterback for Massillon High School (1924–26), whose strongest rival was always Canton McKinley. He went on to play college football at Miami University in Ohio. While there, he also participated on the track team. He coached at Severn Prep School in 1930–31. In 1932, he returned to his alma mater, where he coached for eight years, winning 95 percent of the games. He also coached their reserve team, winning nearly every game.

In 1941 and 1942, he was the head coach at Ohio State. His 1942 Buckeyes were the first ever National Championship team in Ohio State University history. He also coached at Great Lakes Naval Base during WWII in 1944–45.

In 1946, Coach Brown was the first coach and part-owner of the new Cleveland Browns. He was their leader for the next seventeen years, winning nearly 80 percent of the games. He captured four AAFC and three NFL titles and made thirteen post-season appearances. In the ensuing forty years without him, the Browns have close to a 50/50 win-loss record and one championship victory in 1964, and that with almost all of his former players.

Paul Brown's amazing coaching record: 296 wins, 75 losses, 15 ties. Today, he is a member of the Pro Football Hall of Fame.

Brown's greatest gift was his uncanny ability to evaluate talent and to find it in unlikely places. He said, "I want high-grade, intelligent men. I want them strong and lean. There's no place on my team for 'Big Butches' who talk hard and drink hard. I pick my men for good attitudes. I want players who love to win—nobody phlegmatic."

Paul was the first coach to make the sport a full-time business. His coaches and scouts were striving for player perfection. A grading system for players was established. His teams were well-prepared, disciplined, exciting, and competitive. His team was the best in football in every level of the game. Other teams began imitating his example, and the game became better because of it. His teams were always at the top or close to it, but after 1957 he could never quite get over the hump to win another championship.

PAUL AND THE PRESS

Paul wanted to have absolute control. Then he had no one to blame but himself. And he wasn't afraid to take the blame, either. He told one sportswriter after we lost, "I set the defense, I set the offense, I call the plays. Don't blame the players, blame me."

Paul's advice on what players should say to the press: "When you win, say three things. Be short, positive, and compliment the other team. If you lose, say the same three things, but with fewer words."

The press more or less reacted like the players. They had great respect for him. Paul never criticized a reporter. In fact, he went to great lengths to teach them the technical strategies on both offense and defense, believing the press should be informed so the media could write and talk intelligently about football. Some knew the plays as well as the players. They traveled with us and wrote positive or constructive articles.

PAUL'S WISDOM

On Saturdays before games we'd go out on the field, stretch, jog, loosen up, and get a good feel of the game turf. One time in Philadelphia, Paul looks up as we're all coming out of the dugout. There's about twenty workers leaning on their shovels and brooms watching us. It was snowing, and they were supposed to be cleaning the stadium before the game. They're all shouting at us, "Hey, you guys are gonna lose! You bums are gonna lose!" Paul looked at them and said to his team, "Come here, men." We all gathered around him for some worldly knowledge. He said, "Men, I want to give you one word of advice. Never listen to a guy that's leaning on a shovel or broom. He is a loser!" Paul could say more in a few words than anyone I ever knew.

PAUL BROWN DISCIPLINE

No one ever gave excuses or talked back to Paul Brown. Veterans warned everyone immediately—keep your mouth shut except for "No, Sir" and "Yes, Sir."

One time our offensive end dropped a sure touchdown pass, and we lost the game by three points. We're watching game film as a team on the first day back to practice. Coach Brown is operating the film projector, going over and over each play. He comes to the dropped pass and asks, "What happened? How could you drop it?" The end says, "It hit me on the wrist. Coach."

Paul stops the projector, turns on the lights, and says to end, "The ball hit you on the wrist?"

"Yes, Coach."

"Which wrist?"

"The right one."

"Where on the wrist?"

"Here, Coach."

"Oh, the right wrist right here." He holds the end's arm up high so we could all see it. Then he says, "Now point to where on the wrist." The end points. "How far would you say that is to your palm?" "About two inches." Coach to quarterback: "For this week's game, make sure you throw the passes two inches higher so this end can catch it." At the end of the season, that end was traded.

Paul once fined a player for not being on the field for an extra point. He said, "But Coach, I thought I was supposed to be in for field goals only!"

(Despite being a strong disciplinarian, he told his players to call him "Paul" or "Coach." Players never called him Mr. Brown.)

TITHING

Paul was one of the first coaches to have prayer before and after games. He even had a team priest. I still remember Father Connelly traveling with the team. He was a big man, could have played tackle. Father Connelly was at every home and away game. One time Paul went to the Catholic church with him and us players. I'll never forget it because they had three collections during the mass. Paul gave money the first two times, but when the basket came around the third time, I heard him whisper to Father, "What are they going to do now, rob us?" Father started laughing out loud uncontrollably.

BE CAREFUL WHO YOU ASSOCIATE WITH

One Wednesday shortly after practice during my rookie season, Paul Brown saw me in the dressing room laughing and talking to Bob Gain and a few other old-timers. They were telling me about a place they usually stopped to have snacks and brews on their way home. Paul pulled me aside before he left and said, "Schaf, I don't mean to interfere with your personal life, but let me give you a suggestion. Stay away from Bob Gain and his small circle of friends. They don't always go to the best places, and they sometimes associate with questionable people." I was about to say, "Coach, is there anybody you would recommend?" And he added, "I'd like to recommend a real solid type of guy that would be more your type—Walt Michaels." I said, "Okay. Thanks, Coach." So Walt and I agreed to stop at the place he usually stopped on his way home. We parked our cars on a side street, and I followed him through a back door of a bar/restaurant. Lo and behold, sitting at a table is Bob Gain and all the guys Paul had talked about! Walt sat down with them, so I did, too! I was thinking, boy, do they all have Coach fooled. What would he do if he knew the truth? Maybe he did.

PAUL BROWN'S SAYINGS

The worst thing you can do to an opponent is to beat him.

Do a better job each game or I promise you someone else will be in your chair, and soon.

Are you ready? It's your game, win or lose!

On the field or on the bus, you're a Cleveland Brown.

Players nursed on mother's milk at birth have more stamina.

It takes three things to make the Browns a team: Reading, Writing, and Route 71 from Columbus.

It takes one sentence to explain a win; it takes a book to explain a loss.

We'll be as good a football team as the class of people we are.

Don't be afraid to tell your player who is out-of-line or breaking rules that he owes it to his team and school to straighten himself out. You win with everyone pulling together. Never ever allow one player to pull the whole team down.

Preparation is key to winning.

Character is the difference in a close game.

You run on your own fuel—it comes from within.

Four words of advice: Just Show Up Ready.

MORRIE KONO

Morrie Kono came to the Browns in 1948, immediately after being discharged from the army. He signed a deal in one minute to be the Browns' equipment manager. Never asked Paul what his salary was—just needed a job to eat. Morrie did it all. He opened and locked up the training camp facility every day. He worked like a full-time mom for thirty-three men. He took care of the players' laundry. He packed all the uniforms and equipment for every game. He was Paul Brown's appointed spy and detective and enforcer. He answered the clubhouse pay phone and, sometimes, he lied to protect the guilty! He got lunches for the players and coaches at the local diner. He even rode the blocking sled for the offensive line and held the tackling dummies for the defense. At Christmas time, Morrie always put up a tree in the locker room and decorated it with jock straps, socks, and used tape.

Paul Brown was always afraid that someone might have a wire or tape hidden in the pipes or heating vents to listen to us in the locker room. He had Morrie tape every peephole, every crack in the wall, and every vent before practices and games. Nobody could get an edge on him. He always whispered everything in the dressing room. He was well aware of the scruples of some of the opposing coaches.

Just before every game Paul allowed Morrie to perform for us in our dressing room. With only five minutes before we were to go onto the field, Paul would leave the room to meet with the other coaches, and Morrie would jump up in front of the team and mock Paul Brown. He was realistic in his enactment as he walked around the room whispering with both hands cupped around his mouth, "Okay, men, here are the first four plays." Then he'd hold one finger in the air. First play: "Bobby Mitchell around left end." He'd run to the left, stop, and shake his head like there was no gain.

Then, with two fingers to his lips. Second play: "Pass to Leroy Bolden." Leroy was the smallest guy on the team, and Morrie would drop back and pretend to throw the ball down at the ground because Leroy was so short. Again, he'd shake his head in disappointment. For the third play, he's holding up three fingers. "Jim Brown up the middle." After a few quick steps he stops and shakes his head like nothing good happened. Then he'd put up four fingers. He'd drop back and pretend to punt the ball. It was a riot—a perfect parody of Paul. Then the coaches would enter the room. We'd say a prayer and head down the long tunnel toward the crowd and onto the field.

Until 1965, we always practiced in Cleveland's Old League Park, a real relic. We played some games there, too. Babe Ruth, Tris Speaker, Ty Cobb, and many other baseball greats also played there. The park was built in 1891 for the Cleveland Indians. In 1946 the Indians moved to the huge Municipal Stadium, which was built by WPA funds in the Depression years of 1934–35. By the 1950s, the Old League locker room was kinda like an old dungeon with crumbling cement walls. Water buckets were used to catch raindrops that leaked every place. There was a six-inch-deep trough about a foot wide around the outside base of the meeting rooms in case of heavy rains or if you needed to wash the place out. We had our team meetings there during the regular season. The room had twenty-five lockers for thirty-three players and cab members. There were four showers, one toilet, one urinal, one sink, and one trainer's table. Coaches and meeting rooms were on the visitor's side. One pay phone outside. Rats would sometimes eat our chin straps or the ear pads of the helmets.

This one day it was raining cats and dogs, lots of thunder and lightning. We're all sitting here in the dungeon having our meeting when all of a sudden the lights blinked and went out. Paul Brown yells, "Morrie, fix it!" Morrie says, "Okay, Coach." He runs out the door. Across the street are two bars. It's 9:30 in the morning and four winos are already sitting there. Morrie says, "Anybody want to make five bucks?" Two of them follow him back to the park. Morrie's got a flashlight and a light fuse for them. We're sitting in the dark waiting. Water is running in the drains and the whole trough is full. These two guys both step into the water and put the fuse in the electric box. The lights come on and Paul says, "Great job, Morrie!" These guys walk out with their five bucks!

Once when we were practicing at League Park, Paul thought he saw someone (a spy) on a school roof nearby. So he said, "Morrie, check it out!" So Morrie ran over to the schoolhouse and climbed the fire escape to the roof. A janitor was cleaning and sharpening some tools. Morrie told him, "The coach said you're not to watch us practice. Now, go back inside to finish the things you're doing." Paul knew that opposing coaches paid spies to watch the Browns practice.

Another time we were practicing at Hiram College. It's 8 a.m. The players were on the field and Paul spots a parked car about one hundred feet past the far end of the field. Paul says, "Morrie, check it out. It must be a spy." Morrie runs to where the car is parked and sees a guy sound asleep. Morrie knocks on the window and wakes him to ask what's he doing here. The guys says, "I'm a salesman from Chicago, and I arrived early for a ten o'clock appointment and thought I'd get some shut-eye." Morrie says, "You'd better move your car, sir, to another place. The coach doesn't want you to watch practice!"

Another day at Hiram, Paul sees a guy on a pole close to the practice field. "Morrie, go check it out; it's probably a spy." Morrie runs to the pole, talks to the guy—he's an electrician fixing the line.

Morrie tells him, apologetically, "The coach doesn't want you taking any pictures of our practice," and runs back. Paul asked what happened. Morrie said, "It's okay, Coach, he's an electrician working on loose wires." Paul says, "Oh really? I've heard that old chestnut before."

Morrie lived the Paul Brown doctrine and made sure the players did, too. He never complained. He loved his job. His nickname was "Fix It." Morrie died shortly after his retirement in 1990. He set a high standard for future managers to follow.

LEO MURPHY

Our trainer was Leo Murphy. Leo carried both a black satchel bag and a box with a handle. He could fix anything. He was like a traveling druggist, medical doctor, and psychiatrist all rolled into one. He always had tape, tools, smelling salts, and bandages as well as all kinds of pills, turpentine and tar, and, of course, the famous healing towel. If you were in pain or ill, Leo gave you a pill and you were suddenly all right. It didn't matter what he gave you; you just knew it would fix your problem.

Husband, father, self-made trainer, cigar smoker, distinguished piano player, heart and soul of the Cleveland Browns for nearly forty years, Leo was chief counsel, adviser, masseuse, doctor, nurse, and medicine man for all ailments rolled into one. Born in Buffalo, New York, in the mid-1920s, he was a good high school athlete. He earned a basketball scholarship to attend the University of Notre Dame, where he majored in education. Leo always made light of his basketball career by saying that he sat on the bench so much he was called "the Judge."

After graduation in 1948, he found a job with the Studebaker Company at South Bend. But Leo's first love was sports and helping people. Soon he found a part-time job with the old Chicago Rockets of the American Football Conference. The team folded after the 1948 season, unable to attract the same level of attention as its competitors, the Bears and the Cardinals.

Through friends and associates, Leo and his wife Betty ended up in New York. He was trainer for both Casey Stengel and the Yankees and Red Stroder and the Giants. In 1959, Wally Bock, trainer of both the Browns and Indians, retired from the Browns to just work for the Tribe. Leo was looking for a way to get out of the Big Apple when he heard of the Browns opening. Paul offered Leo the trainer's job. Leo accepted.

When Leo arrived in Cleveland, he expected to work part-time with Studebaker, but they immediately went on strike. A few weeks later, he was hired by Blepp Combs Sporting Goods Company. He always carried everything he needed for both jobs in his station wagon. Leo retired as Browns trainer in 1989 after nearly forty years. Today he's in the Trainers Hall of Fame in Dallas, Texas.

FRITZ HEISLER AND EDDIE ULINSKI, LINE COACHES

Fritz Heisler molded great offensive lines in the 1940s, '50s, and '60s—the best in pro ball. He was the master doing his thing until the end of Blanton Collier's era in 1971.

Fritz and his trusted friend Coach Eddie Ulinski were two loyal, tough hombres. They spent most of their adult lives coaching and helping the Cleveland Browns. Fritz was a little guy—stood five foot five and weighed about 150 pounds. His players towered over him. He was always standing on his toes in front of linemen looking up into their faces, yelling or talking loudly, with his thick, steel-rimmed glasses sliding down his nose.

Eddie was about six feet tall and 180 pounds. He played tackle for the original Browns in the 1940s. He assisted Fritz with the offensive tackles and doing all the film work so we could study films.

No one could out-work or out-tough these guys. Thanks to them, we were the best offensive line in professional football during the '60s, putting three backs into the NFL Hall of Fame (Mitchell, Brown, and Kelly).

Fritz Heisler's twenty-five-year tenure included some amazing statistics: twenty-one years in post-season games; eight AAFC and four NFL championships; six second-place world championships; and seventeen post-season games, with only one losing season.

LOYALTY OF STAFF

Almost every assistant coach under Paul Brown stayed with him forever. I've mentioned Fritz Heisler and Eddie Ulinski, but Howard Brinker and Dub Jones were also with him. They stayed with the Browns 'til they retired. Each team had five assistants! Paul Brown's assistants stayed with Blanton Collier. It was a very loyal staff. It gave the Browns stability.

At one time there were forty-five assistant coaches and twenty-one head coaches in the NFL who had previously coached or played for Paul Brown.

I'M IN THE NFL NOW

In 1959, during intra-squad practice scrimmage at Hiram College, I was standing on the sidelines as a rookie watching. Behind me, my family and friends were yelling, "We want Schafrath! We want Schafrath!" I strolled over close to Coach Brown and said, "What do you think, Coach?" He said, "I think since they want you so bad, you should go sit with them."

Nobody ever got real close to Paul. His eyes did the talking. I was always taught to respect a person in authority and the wisdom of older people. Paul was wise and in charge. He wasted few words. All players adapted quickly to everything that he wanted. He was very demanding, very structured, very organized, very disciplined, and very controlling. Practices were to the minute, never over one hour. He had this clock on the practice field that rang every five minutes. It was timed for us to change units. Each day he did the same things—basics and fundamentals. He kept it simple, and I liked that. All work and no horsing around. Football is a game of emotion, and Paul left the mental preparation up to you. If you couldn't prepare and motivate yourself, you weren't around very long. Also, if you weren't a team player, you had a short stay. He insisted on loyalty, remembering your roots, class-act people, and staying out of trouble.

We did everything as a team on and off the field. We even helped teammates move and build their houses.

Paul loved seeing wives and kids come to camp on special family days. And he always wanted you looking good. Think of your image first! He always stressed, "You are what your foundation shows. Your image will reflect the class of players that are on our team." He wanted you to shine your shoes. In fact, once in a while I would notice that my socks were different colors, and that wasn't good. He made an impression on me, and I shined my shoes more often than I ever had before. I still talk to a lot of people who say they really respected Paul because his guys always showed up in a shirt and tie, and never smoked or drank in front of kids while on public appearances. Paul said daily, "We are to be a good example and represent the Cleveland Browns with pride." Between Woody and Paul, they helped change my image somewhat. My mom always said, "You can take the boy off the farm, but not the farm out of the boy!"

I never had a new suit until I came to the Browns. All the players would go to Richman Brothers, where they had deals for players wanting a new tailor-made suit. I had no idea what "tailored" meant. First suit—$20. I never asked questions, but I knew Paul had made arrangements. It fit just like it was supposed to. Conveniently, Morrie Kono had a friend (Phil Hertz) who owned Bobbie Brooks, a women's clothing line in Cleveland. All the wives and daughters got great clothing for bargains there. These were perks we really appreciated considering our salaries those days.

Paul gave me a choice the first day of practice: I could play center, left guard, or left offensive tackle. I don't know why I chose tackle. At that time, the defenses were mostly a four-three and nobody was ever over the center. That position didn't sound like there was much action. I later realized the center had more freedom than any of the other linemen. He could be helping a teammate or trapping or racing after linebackers downfield. The center just needed to have twinkle toes so his feet weren't stepped on in all the heavy traffic. When I got out there on the end of the line as a tackle, there was usually the fastest, biggest, meanest guy on the defense. That was war, every play one-on-one, and that's where I wanted to be.

I didn't play much as a regular my first year with the Browns. I was mainly a backup for all line positions—both on offense and defense, and as a starter on all special teams. All teams had one extra lineman. With a total of thirty-three players, there were eleven extras to back up all twenty-two of the opposing positions. Every week in our Tuesday morning meeting, Coach Brown insisted that we all write down every word he had to say about all twenty-two players we were to face for the coming game. A few older veterans didn't do it, but most of us did. Paul certainly wasn't going to catch me not writing everything down. In fact, a few guys who took a lot of notes each Tuesday later became great coaches.

During my first and second year on the Browns, I was locked in all-out battle, competing for the starting left tackle position with Willie Davis (Packers), Jim Marshall (Vikings), Jim Houston (Browns), and Fran O'Brien (Redskins). Lou Groza (Browns) became kicker only. Somehow, I won out and was the starter for the next twelve years. I learned from some outstanding older linemen, including Groza, McCormick, Hickerson, Chuck Noll, and Jim Ray Smith. All were future Hall of Famers or Pro Bowlers. Future NFL coaches from Paul Brown's roster were Chuck Noll, Mike McCormack, John Sandusky, Paul Wiggin, Don Shula, Floyd Peters, Vince Costello, Monte Clark, Ara Parseghian, Alex Agasse, Mac Speedie, Abe Gibron, and a host of others. Later, when I coached with George Allen and the Redskins, I used that same old Browns playbook for reference. Blanton Collier was amazing, too. Anybody who grew up in the Paul Brown/Blanton Collier era knew the techniques to all twenty-two positions. These coaches taught you fundamentals backwards and forwards, and they made you write them and memorize them until they became habit. You were able to teach them, too.

MY FIRST GAME WITH THE BROWNS

The first game I started as a Brown was against the Steelers and their All Pro defensive end Ernie Stautner. I had been coached by Lou Groza for weeks that on the first pass play. I was confident and ready. I got down in my stance and listened for the starting count. Stautner was saying some real unpleasant things about my mom and family. I wasn't too worried, though; Groza had showed me a hundred times how to be like a boxer and duck that first blow. When the ball was snapped, I knew Lou had forgotten to tell me one thing: Stautner was left-handed. I ducked the wrong way, and he hit me big time and followed up with seven more hits. Boy, was my bell ringing as I went reeling backwards with each hit. Paul Brown replaced me with Groza for a couple of series so I could recover. I finally went up to Paul and said, "Coach, please let me back in. I want to play in the worse way." He said, "I know, Schaf. That's why you're not playing."

My second year I weighed in at 275. I was really confident. I was the biggest guy on the team, offensive or defense, for next five years. I could eat like a mule and get paid for it. During training camp in 1960, Paul wanted to help me gain weight, so he gave me a key to the cafeteria for all-night service. I never abused the privilege. There was no one spying or there to question me if I did.

THE WAY IT WAS

From the 1920s through the 1960s, all professional players had an off-season job to support themselves and their families. Full-time off-season jobs could continue during regular season as there was no practice on Mondays and Tuesdays, and practice was over by 2:30 p.m. on Wednesdays, Thursdays, and Fridays. No one worked out in off-season. Many excellent players retired early in their career because they could not survive on their football salaries. Records and statistics meant nothing.

During the football season, all the Browns players traveled to and from ball games together. We were required to be dressed in suits, shirts and ties. We traveled on busses, trains or prop-driven planes, with players in front; coaches, officials, sportswriters, and broadcasters to the rear. Different order in the buses—white starters and the head coach rode on the first bus; black players and everyone else rode the second bus.

SALARY NEGOTIATIONS

During my football career, I held construction jobs, helped on the farm, sold insurance, sold swimming pools, helped develop a sports camp, and served in the U.S. Air Force and Air National Guard. I was also a part-time postal carrier. Had public relations jobs with Canada Dry, Cleveland Plumbing Industry, and the Cleveland Police. I often worked several jobs at a time. Both Paul Brown and Art Modell were stubborn in giving me salary raises. They'd say, "Jim Brown doesn't make that kind of money you're asking, Mike McCormick doesn't make that kind of money, Lou Groza doesn't make that kind of money." I'd say, "Okay, but some new rookies are making more money than any of us. My blocking grades are high. You've got to treat me differently." They'd both say, "No, no, we can't do that. We'd go broke giving you the kind of money you're asking for." Boy, were they tough! Most players before 1970 had short careers because they pursued better-paying jobs.

THE THIRTEENTH CHECK

All players got paid each week during the twelve weeks of the season. But Paul gave thirteen payments. Just in case you had a bill that needed to be paid after the season ended, the thirteenth check paid creditors!

Before the 1970s Paul insisted that nobody knew what anyone else was making. Some players, like myself, were too embarrassed to tell anyone anyway—we weren't making enough to brag. Paul tried to keep wives apart at games, as he didn't want them sharing personal information about things like salaries. Today you can call the league office and get a printout of the whole team's salaries in a matter of minutes.

Even when I became a state senator, I didn't know how much my salary was. Money has never been the number one objective in my life, but I think that once a person proves himself or herself and does well, he or she should be paid fairly. I believe in the incentive plan. Unlike most players, I thought I could play forever and eventually work my way up to being a millionaire. Yeah, right! But, I found out soon—you can't play forever, and not everything in life is fair.

FOOTBALL SALARIES THEN AND NOW

1. Team Budget 1964: For players, coaches, and front-office personnel. Total cost—less than $1 million
2. Team Budget 2004: For players, coaches, and front-office personnel. Total cost—approximately $75 million
3. Average salaries for players in 1964: $22,000
4. Average salaries for players in 2004: $1.285 million
5. One good player's salary today would equal the entire payroll of half of the NFL teams in the 1960s.

HELMET EXPERIMENTS

For most of my professional career I never had a helmet that fit me right. The helmets were constantly changing. All players had some problems. During the 1950s and '60s it was a constant experiment. I started with the leather helmet in high school, went to no face mask to plastic helmet with suspension, then to face mask. At Ohio State it was a single bar. Then with the Browns a double bar, then triple bar, then a bar down the middle of all three bars. Then an air-pocket helmet, then a water-pocket helmet, then back to a suspension-only helmet. The worst was the air and water period. After the defensive end would bang my head a couple of times, I'd start losing air or water from the helmet pockets. The pockets, maybe one hundred of them, were 1" x 1", and some would just pop after a good head hit. After a half dozen plays, my helmet was half deflated and would become loose. It would start spinning like a top. I'd come to the sidelines, where they'd pump me up with air or water. If the damage was too bad, they would throw me another helmet. By half time I was sometimes using one hand to hold my helmet on straight while using the other arm or shoulder to block.

HEAD SLAPS

I can't be more sincere when I say this—unless you played the offensive line position in 1950s and '60s, you can't begin to understand how vicious the head slap was. Most defensive linemen would tape their hands until they were twice as big as normal. Some of us thought that, at times, there was something hard under the tape, too. When they first popped you, your helmet would rattle for two or three seconds. Boy, would it sting. Your head and helmet were ringing all the time. You couldn't defend against it because the rules said that the offensive lineman couldn't have his hands extended like he can today. You had to be kidding me—just stick my head out and say "hit me"? It didn't make much sense.

From the head slaps, I developed three herniated disks in my neck area—real bad! My last couple years in the league I could feel the sting from nerve burns sometimes from my neck to my toes. Over the past thirty-plus years since retiring, the burns have weakened, but every once in awhile I still have a bad pinch. When I played in the later years of my career, I'd wear a neck collar to try and cushion the blows. Sometimes while running, I would suddenly fall to the ground paralyzed for a second from the nerve burn. In the late 1970s, the vicious head slap was finally outlawed.

The NFL Players Association did a survey about neck and head problems a few years ago. I haven't seen the results, but it was all about the effects of head concussions, head slaps, and artificial playing surfaces on players. I always say getting hit in the head for twenty years had one positive: It prepared me to be a state senator.

Hall of Famer Ernie Stautner of the Steelers was probably the greatest headhunter of all times. He was like blocking a Coke machine, and his fists felt like barbells when he hit you. He drove me crazy! He'd smile or complain to the official to keep watching me so I wouldn't hold. Besides Stautner, I faced three other Hall of Famers each year: Robustelli, Bethea, and Atkins. I know they're all there thanks to my performance against them. All Pros I played against were Lamar Lundy (Rams), George Andrie (Cowboys), Ordell Brasse (Colts), Ben Davidson (Raiders), Luke Owens (Cardinals), Jim Marshall (Vikings), and Lyle Alzado (Broncos).

A couple years ago when Doug Atkins came to a Browns reunion, I asked him how big he actually was when he played. He said he was six foot seven, 290 pounds. At the University of Tennessee, he played basketball and high-jumped seven feet in a track meet. If you tried to cut him, he'd fly right over you. You had to try to stay up in his face as long as you could. I asked him to name the toughest guy he ever played against. He said, "Nobody!" I thought maybe he'd say me. I always welcomed help from Ernie Green on pass protection when playing against Doug or any of those other great ends. Ernie was an outstanding team player and an All Pro—kinda like having a coach on the field with you. Ernie and I still laugh about Doug Atkins. I'd be saying, "Ernie, I need help. You're going to help me right? You take inside and I'll take outside, right? Huh, Ernie?" "Okay, Schaf." I finally came up with a three-step plan on how to block Atkins on a pass play. (1) Hit him as hard as I could in his chest with my helmet and right fist; (2) Throw a hip, knee, and shoe at his groin area as I hit him with my left fist; (3) Try to grab hold of one of his ankles as he was jumping over me.

It was the same thing for Monte Clark, our right tackle, when he was playing across from Deacon Jones, Willie Davis, Gino Marchetti, or Carl Eller. Of course, John Wooten and Gene Hickerson, our guards, would always be calling for help, too. Our center, John Morrow, would be helping the one who yelled the loudest. Each of us would always argue we had the toughest guy.

BROWNS TRADITION FOR ROOKIES

During training camp each summer, at dinner time, or immediately before meetings, a veteran would call out a rookie's name. The rookie had to stand, state his name, put his hand over his heart, and sing his college fight song. Depending on how good the applause was, he was either rewarded with a beverage at a local pub or forced to do some stupid task like sing it again or carry a veteran's playbook for a few days. I always sang "Fight the Team Across the Field." I still love the words.

WHAT'S PAIN?

Everyone played football with a lot of pain. In the early days you played or no pay. I remember one time our offensive end, Gern Nagler, came to the sidelines. He had a broken nose. Paul Brown said, "Hey Nagler, what are you doing here?" Gern's nose was bent flat to his cheek and bleeding. He says, "My nose, Coach. I think it's broke. " Coach says, "A broken nose? You're here because of a broken nose?" Gern says, "But Coach, it won't stop bleeding!" Paul quickly summoned Leo Murphy, who wrapped tape around Gern's nose and helmet five or six times, then sent him back onto the field. He played the rest of the first half. They repaired him at halftime, and he was okay.

One time John Morrow had his fibula bone sticking out of the calf area of his sock. In the huddle it looked bad and was bleeding. We kept saying, "John, get the heck off the field! You're crazy. You need medical help." He said, "Nope, I'm not getting out of here until we score!"

Otto Graham had his face smashed into a bench in the second quarter. It took forty stitches to sew him up at halftime. He played the second half, and the Browns won!

Gary Collins played with cracked ribs. He could hardly breathe or bend over to get in stance, but he still played.

Players played with broken bones, jaws, cheekbones, ribs, fingers, toes. Dislocated shoulders, hips, elbows, knees. The trainers knew how to jerk them back into place, glue them, tape them, and numb them so they'd be playing the next series. If they were shaken up mentally, trainers put smelling salts to the nose. If the salts didn't open your head and clean the cobwebs from a good hit, then you were probably dead!

We were battling the Pittsburgh Steelers when I received a knee to the helmet. I saw stars and laid on the ground in a daze. Time out was called by the officials. Leo Murphy and our physician Vic

Ippolito ran onto the field. I remember smelling some kind of powerful stuff Leo had stuffed into my nose. He was saying, "Are you okay, Schaf? Can you hear me? How many fingers?" Finally, I got to my knees, then he and Doc helped me stand up. In a couple of minutes I was fine. Doc said, "Feel good enough to continue?" "Sure do, I'm ready to go." Then I turned to Doc. "Hey, Leo." "Yeah, Schaf. What?" "How's the crowd taking it?" They both said, "He sounds normal. Go get 'em, Mule!"

GIVING IT MY ALL AND GETTING SOME IN RETURN

The first couple years, Paul criticized my performance a lot, but I kept working hard and tried not to get too discouraged. Any coach that isn't on you to get better is usually not interested in you. One time, this guy who played for the Redskins said in the paper, "I can't wait to play over that Schafrath." I did some good things against him during the game, and Paul stopped the film a few times on the following Tuesday and said, "Hey Schaf, that's the guy who couldn't wait to get a piece of you!" He always came up with a word to encourage me, too.

Paul stuck with me. Eddie Ulinski and Fritz Heisler would call me once in a while the night before a practice and say, "Schaf, I just want to warn you. Paul's going to be singling you out today. You didn't look too good on some plays." Then they'd add, "You should be okay, though. You're just learning and doing a lot of good things."

It wasn't like you had a real ongoing, friendly relationship with Paul. He kept you at a distance and worried to death. It was a fear that he would embarrass you in front of your teammates. If he did, you just took it like a man because he did it with everybody except his staff, Jim Brown and Lou Groza, who were exempt. As we watched film together, he'd go back and forth over a play four or five times, and if he felt like saying something, he would: "Boy, that's a good blow there," or "You're killing us." If you were the one "killing us" too often, you were gone.

A lot of your fears were that he would not say anything. He'd tell you he was going to look at your notebook, and if you didn't have everything written down, there was going to be a $50 fine. If you didn't have your notebook in your locker, it would cost another $50. If you were one minute late, it would cost you $50 and an additional $50 for every fifteen minutes. If you were late for anything, fines. Everybody was always early. I was never fined. I only know one guy who was. At the football events, it was called "Paul Brown's Time." You were always in your seat at least fifteen minutes early.

Just when you are thinking, "I don't know if this guy even likes me," the human side of Paul would surface. He'd say something nice to you about your performance, and you'd feel like a million bucks. He knew the right time to do that. With Woody and Blanton, it was almost daily. With Paul, it might take a week or so. He'd suddenly be aware that there was a little tension going on and he'd say something. Of course, he got rid of the players he didn't like. If he was going to cut you, he never told you directly. He'd call two or three names out at a team meeting and tell them to pick up an envelope in the morning. One guy would be cut—the other two would be okay. Nobody ever knew who was to be cut.

HISTORY AND INTEGRATION

To understand what a thrill it was for me to play for the Cleveland Browns, you've got to know a bit about football history.

Football was big in Ohio almost from the beginning. In 1903, football officially migrated to Ohio from Pennsylvania, and many city athletic clubs quickly sprung up across the Buckeye State. Ohio's first pro team was the Massillon Tigers, based in a city twenty miles east of my hometown. Their arch rival quickly became next-door neighbor the Canton Bulldogs. Both recruited All-Americans from colleges and even college coaches who played under fictitious names on Sundays. It's no surprise that the Professional National Football Hall of Fame is located in Canton.

Early football was not for sissies. Each team had about fifteen players and few, if any, time-outs. There was no forward passing, and most of the offensive plays consisted of a "flying wedge," players locked together arm in arm while attacking. The ball carrier was not "down" until he could no longer move and yelled, "I give up." There seldom was an off sides call, and players did not wear much in the way of pads and helmets. You could block an opponent in the back, below the knees, or spear him with your head. Quarterbacks were fair game—no protection from any kind of hit. Players never left the field until the game was over or until they were carried off. My heroes were greats like Greasy Neale and Knute Rockne of the University of Notre Dame; Red Grange, a three-time All-American from Illinois; and Bronko Nagurski, an All-American from Minnesota at two positions, fullback and tackle. All played for the Massillon and Canton teams. My love for the legendary Fighting Irish seven mules and four horsemen lead to my being nicknamed "Mule."

For hours as a youngster, I practiced the popular but difficult dropkick for making extra points. The use of a spotting tee for placekicks replaced the dropkick in the mid-1940s. It resurfaced temporarily in 2005, when Doug Flutie of the New England Patriots successfully dropkicked an extra point after a touchdown in their last regular season game.

The first black person I ever saw was during a Hot Stove League baseball game in Wooster when I was ten years of age. Soon after, my family met his family at our church. And a short while later, I had a black teammate on our high school football team. As a kid, I loved reading stories about blacks and Indians. They were my heroes. Jim Thorpe was my favorite Indian. Jack Johnson was my favorite black.

The first known black professional football player, Charles W. Follis, the "Black Cyclone," was from my hometown of Wooster. He helped organize Wooster High School's first football team in 1899. That's the same team would play on fifty years later. Now there's a stadium in Wooster name Follis Field.

When Follis turned pro in 1904, he played for an athletic club in Shelby, Ohio. His roommate was none other than Branch Rickey. Mr. Rickey later served as general manager of the Brooklyn Dodgers and integrated major league baseball when he signed Jackie Robinson in 1947.

In 1946, the Browns had three outstanding black players: Bill Willis, Marion Motley, and Horace Gillum. Willis and Motley are NFL Hall of Famers. They helped lead Cleveland to ten straight championship seasons. The Browns were one of the first NFL teams that offered blacks the opportunity to play since the early 1920s. Paul Brown didn't care what color a guy's skin was as long as he could run, catch, block, or tackle.

When I started playing football in 1951, there were few blacks playing with or against whites in any sport. I played against two really great black athletes in high school, Warner Harper at Orrville and Jim Roseboro of Ashland. Roseboro later became a good halfback for the 1954–55 Buckeyes. At Ohio State, I had several outstanding black teammates and team leaders: NFL Hall of Fame, Jim Parker, Leo Brown and Don Clark (both team captains), Bill Cummings, Aurelius Thomas, Ernie Wright, Jim Marshall, Bertho Arnold, and Phil Robinson.

Unbelievable as it seems, during the 1950s and '60s there were still many separate race rules in cities with regards to buses, restaurants, and hotels. In 1963, former Browns teammate and Hall of Famer Bobby Mitchell was the first black athlete to play football for the Washington Redskins.

Today, high school, college, and professional teams are loaded with great black stars. It's hard to imagine a time when they were a rarity.

Paul Brown and Woody Hayes always stressed team first. Winners played *together*. But sometimes the rules of society didn't work in our favor. We had outside resistance to whites and blacks eating or sleeping together. Some blacks had to stay with local black families. Early on, teams had even numbers of white and black players so everyone would have a roommate of the same color.

I figured that my teammates had to work equally as hard as I did to make the team. Nobody had given them anything—they earned it.

CHAPTER FIVE

TEAMMATES AND FRIENDS

FRAN O'BRIEN VISITS THE MULE'S FARM

In 1959, after a home game in late October, I took Fran O'Brien to Wooster to stay overnight at my parents' farm. Franie was drafted out of Michigan State by the Browns the same year I was, in 1958. Both of us were tackles. Both of us played in the College All-Star game together. He was traded to the Redskins after our first season. When he left I really missed him. He was the only person I ever met that would throw away his shirts, socks, and underwear rather than wash them. He kept me stocked with those important items. He was from Holyoke, Massachusetts, and since he had never been on a farm, he wanted to see where I grew up.

As soon as we got to the farm, I received orders to go to Mansfield and report to my Air National Guard unit. Since I had to stay there overnight, I told Dad to take care of Franie for me.

Dad dressed Fran in his farm bib overalls, straw hat, and manure boots, and initiated him immediately to farm life. All Fran really wanted was a case of cold beer, a pool table, and maybe a girl to do a little dancing and jiving. But Dad kept Fran at his side every minute—helping to gather eggs, milking the cows, pitching hay, feeding the mules, pigs, and chickens, cutting firewood, cutting and shocking corn.

Fran was exhausted. He'd never been exposed to manual labor like that before.

As I drove back to the farm from Mansfield the next morning, I noticed Fran in the cornfield. When he saw me coming down the road he immediately started racing at full gallop across the cornfield towards my car. The first thing he said was, "Schaf, your dad's crazy! You got to get me out of here. He's nuts! All he does is work, work, work, and I'm full of cow's milk! He drinks it by the gallon. I need a beer! A hot shower!" I laughed at him all dressed up in Dad's farm clothes. Then he took off his straw cap and showed me how Dad had scalped him, the quick two-minute haircut. Until the day he died, Fran still talked about his experience at Dad's "boot camp"

FRAN O'BRIEN'S FIRST CAR

One day after practice Fran says to me, "Schaf, come and see my new car." The dealer was about two blocks up the street from the hotel where we were rooming. The salesman greets us at the door and says, "Here are your keys for your new car, Mr. O'Brien—enjoy it." Fran is proudly showing me every little bit of it inside and out. Opens the hood—"This is the engine and battery." He opens and shuts all the doors. He pushes the button that makes the windows go up and down. It even has an AM/FM radio. Finally he opens the driver's door and says, "You drive." I say, "No, it's your car. You drive." We're going back and forth when he says, "Schaf, I can't drive. I've never driven and I have no license." I say, "You mean to say you bought this car and don't know how to drive it?" Yep, and even worse it was a stick shift.

So for the next four hours we practiced and practiced. He finally did learn to drive on his own. Four months later, he finally got a license. Fran let every member of the team drive his car any place they wanted to go. He had a great heart.

SAM MORGAN, TOP COOK

In 1961 and 1962, my Air Guard reserve unit was activated into the regular U.S. Air Force because of the Berlin and Cuban crisis. I was on twenty-four-hour alert to be prepared to leave, but because my unit was stationed so close to Cleveland I was still allowed to play football games on Sundays—if the opposing owner said I could. Paul Brown would send me the game plans on Mondays, and I would drive (usually with a friend from our unit) to the games on Saturday night after my normal eight-hour military duty was finished. Say we played Pittsburgh. Paul would send me the plan for how they were going to practice that week, and then on Wednesday he'd overnight-mail me what our short list for Friday would be. I never practiced with the team for two of those years, but I played all the games but one. I'd drive my car to the game, then go back to the base immediately afterwards. When I arrived in Mansfield, I had my regular eight hours to serve. I was usually still wound up from the ball game. As an air policeman, I'd normally drive about five or six miles patrolling the air base during an eight-hour stint. One night after getting back from a game, I drove three hundred miles around the base. After that, my superior officer made me walk the patrol or serve at the main gate after a game.

I drove every place—New York, St. Louis, Washington, Philadelphia. Once, when we were to play Detroit, Coach Brown forgot to leave my ticket at "will call." I had to pay both my way and my driver's way into the game. The friend who drove along with me was Airman Third Class Sam Morgan. Sam was a cook and I worshipped cooks, especially good ones, and he knew how I loved food. Sam is one of the funniest guys I know. He was born in a two-room log cabin, five miles from Hyden, Kentucky, deep in eastern Appalachian country. What a success story. When he was five, his two brothers and two sisters were bussed from Hyden to Dayton, Ohio, with each of them carrying their clothes in a "poke bag." His brothers became outstanding athletes and coaches. Sam was a hustler and practical jokester. People called him a little shady. He sold milk in bottles from door-to-door in mornings and shined shoes outside restaurants and nightclubs the rest of the day and evening.

Anyway, for one game Sam and I drove four hours to Detroit. I promised him he could watch the game from the bench. I introduced him to Paul Brown as "Captain" Morgan. Lo and behold, the game was being televised regionally, including back home to Cleveland. Paul Brown was talking on TV before the game and said, "It's good to have Dick Schafrath here playing with us tonight. Also, I'd like you all to meet Captain Morgan, who was nice enough to drive him here." Sam could have been court-martialed for impersonating an officer. While Paul is trying to find him to be introduced, Sam was hiding behind the bench under a warm-up coat with a hood up over his head.

GARY COLLINS

Gary Collins was also known as Futz or Mr. Clutch (for great pass-catching ability). I always warmly referred to him as Futz. One time he and I were traveling by car on a long trip. At 6'4", 215 pounds, you'd think he had a regular bladder size, but he didn't. It was small. Anyway, after an hour or so of driving towards Cincinnati he starts going into one of his bathroom panic attacks: legs crossed, moaning, groaning, squirming, and yelling for me to make an emergency stop. While he's carrying on, I'm laughing so much that I miss the turn-off to next pit stop. Now he's got to hold it for another twenty minutes. He's threatening me and going crazy. "Please, Schaf, I'm hurting bad!" Several minutes later I'm still coasting to a stop when he bolts out the door and races for restroom. I was standing outside the building stretching and waiting for about five minutes. Finally here he comes with a big happy smile on his face. I decided to go to the bathroom myself. As I was coming in the door, two guys were talking about this guy that had just left. One said, "Never in my life have I heard or witnessed someone so happy going to the bathroom."

Futz was probably the most misunderstood person I ever met, but to me he was easy to figure out. He didn't like to be lied to, and he didn't like being used. You had to gain his trust. And he wasn't afraid to tell you so. If I was ever asked to choose sides for all the Browns I ever played with, he'd be in my top two or three. He's a winner. Unselfish and loyal—what you see is what you get. He always came ready to play. He could do it all—run, block, punt, pass, catch passes, and score touchdowns. A perfectionist, he worked hard at his trade. At one time he scored a touchdown in thirteen straight games. He never had a punt blocked. He sacrificed a lot for the team, and he could play hurt. If he was playing today he'd be averaging at least a dozen catches a game. He did things at the spur of the moment. After scoring a touchdown, he once turned and punted the ball into the end zone crowd.

In practice, Gary marched to his own drumbeat. Sometimes while we were practicing runs on team play he would still be working on his pass patterns to perfect his skills. Woody Hayes coached him in an All-Star game and benched him for not practicing the way he thought he should. Gary still was the star of the game. He deserves a lot of credit towards making our great offense click and has definitely earned his place in the Pro Football Hall of Fame.

THE BEATLES

After football practice one day, Gary Collins and I were invited by my good friend Joe Madigan to a press party before the premier of a new sensational musical group. We were to come to a hotel in downtown Cleveland by 5:30 p.m. Wearing our casual clothes as we walked into the private reception area, we met Joe. He said, "Good, you're a few minutes early. I think you'll enjoy meeting these guys."

The name of the group was The Beatles. They were making their first swing across America. All of a sudden there was a lot of commotion, and into the room came four long-haired guys with a mob of people—mostly security and hosts. Gosh, they looked small. Joe started introducing Gary, and I suddenly got the urge to grab two of them and bench-press them above my head. To everyone's amazement, I did this with little effort, holding them there as they laughed for a few seconds before letting them back down. At that time, I could bench-press over four hundred pounds.

I could never remember which two they were. Joe always told me when I asked, but he died about twenty years ago. Never even thought about whether there was a picture taken. Wow, that would have been something.

FEED MY MAN, HE'S HUNGRY

There was a restaurant on the east side of Cleveland called The Bluegrass. Once I went there with Gary. We both lived in the same development in Aurora, Ohio, and always drove to practice together. I'd drive him nuts. He didn't really care to eat much, so he'd watch me and cheer me on. One day after practice we stopped by The Bluegrass. They had a special going—all you could eat for $10. They saw us coming and offered me $50 to leave! Gary got his usual cup of coffee and said to our waitress, "Feed my man—he's hungry." Afterwards they wrote down everything I ate and had it hanging on the wall for years. I had five bags of clams and five triple-shrimp cocktails to start with. A gallon of milk, a bottle of wine, and I don't know how many Cokes to use as chasers. Then I had a dozen lobster tails and twelve chicken halves with all the trimmings. Gary kept saying, "Waitress, feed my man. He's hungry!" After an hour and a half, they said, "Okay, Schafrath, it's time to go. Your time's up." Gary is still going, "Feed my man. He's hungry!" I said, "Wait, we can't leave yet." They said, "Why?" I said, "We haven't had dessert." The owners, Larry Maiko and Scott Reed, pushed us out the door.

MR. BASKETBALL

John Havlicek may be the best football player who never played in the NFL. Of course, he was a basketball star at Ohio State and went on to be a Hall of Fame player with the Boston Celtics in the NBA. But "Hondo" was drafted and tried out with the Browns in 1962, never having played a down in college.

Havlicek would spellbind us in practice. At six foot six, he was taller than most any defensive back, and he had huge hands. He was in great shape and could run pass routes with the best of them. If a pass was off target or short, he'd reach out with a big hand and haul it in like a basketball.

That year John roomed with Gary Collins, another rookie receiver. It got down to the day before Paul Brown would have to make the final cut. Only one of them was going to make the team. Hondo asked Gary if he was nervous. Gary looked at him and said, "No, and I'm sorry, friend, but you're the one who is going to be cut." Hondo said, "How do you know?" Gary said, "I have a three-year guaranteed no-cut contract." Sure enough, the next day Hondo was cut.

Paul would have made a spot for Havlicek on the Browns but felt he would be sacrificing a great basketball career. Paul said, "You can be a great basketball player, but I'm not sure you could be that great in football. I would advise you to go into basketball, but you can stay with us if you want to give it a try." Hondo decided to take Paul's advice. The rest is history.

BRAVE MEN

In October 1960, we were to play the New York Giants at Yankee Stadium. We were staying at the Commodore Hotel, an older hotel within walking distance of Yankee Stadium, the night before the game. I got into the elevator on the sixth floor with about six Browns teammates. We were going down to a scheduled meeting on the ground floor. A wealthy looking woman, at least eighty years old, got on the elevator with us at the fourth floor. As the elevator started to move again, we heard this big CRASH above our heads. Suddenly, you could feel the elevator jerking and then free falling. We were all scared and yelling. Then the elevator car hit hard as it bottomed out. We all fell to the floor in a pile. The elevator was bouncing a little, the lights went out, and dust was everywhere. When everything settled, you could see about two feet of space into the lobby. We all scrambled to get out as fast as they could. Thank God no one was hurt.

As we looked back at the elevator we noticed a crowd had quickly gathered. The little old lady was still there. In our haste to save ourselves, we had left her! Her hat was off and she looked a little disheveled, but some people managed to pull her out. We were all apologizing. She said, "No big deal," brushed herself off and left in a cab like nothing happened.

GENE HICKERSON

My roommate for thirteen years was Gene Hickerson, our outstanding right offensive guard. He loved to do crossword puzzles by the hours. Gene always brought his own air conditioner to training camp. We had the only one. Everyone else, even I, was too cheap to get one. We always had a lot of teammates visiting our room to cool off. We had to put up a "No Trespassing" sign when we wanted to rest.

After an early unsuccessful marriage, Gene became a lifelong bachelor. Still, all the players' wives loved him. A great practical joker, he loved playing with kids. Everybody knew he dated, but no one ever saw him with anyone. When asked about it, he'd give everyone the same standard answer: "I just found the right one, and we'll get married next month." That was forty years ago. He shared with me a few stories about a girl he knew who also dated Browns' owner Art Modell. Art loved massages, especially foot. I'll let it go at that.

Gene went to college at Ole Miss. He was from Memphis, Tennessee. We had some fun times playing in the Pro Bowl together, six times in California. After the game, we'd always go to Las Vegas for a few days. A gentleman named Texas in charge of celebrities and athletes. He always took good care of us with free rooms, casino games, and shows. Gene had a few friends who grew up in Memphis with Elvis Presley. They were Elvis's bodyguards, and Gene introduced me and a few other teammates to them and Elvis. I remember thinking, gosh, Elvis looks kinda small. I always thought he had long legs. At least, it looked that way when he shook them to music on TV. His eyes looked penetrating and competitive. Elvis loved Jim Brown. Gene arranged for Art to send him some of our Browns game films so he could study Jim running in slow motion.

The night before games I'd always get pretty nervous and have a hard time getting to sleep. Gene would be calmly working his crossword puzzles and watching late-night TV. I sometimes had to take a sleeping pill to get some rest.

One night I took a pill and got into a deep sleep. I dreamed I died and, because of my sins, was told by St. Peter to go down below for awhile. The ugly devil was standing there in his red suit holding a pitchfork in front of a fiery pit. As he started nudging me to move forward, I decided no way—too hot! I reached behind me and threw a guy into the pit. The devil tried to poke me again, and I threw another in the pit. After the third time, Hickerson's shaking me and shouting, "Schaf, you try to throw me out of my bed one more time and I'm going to knock the hell out of you!" I gave him a thankful nudge and went back to sleep.

One night during training camp just before bed check, someone was screaming and racing down the hall. All doors were bursting open to see what was happening. Bobby Mitchell was sprinting a 4-second 40-yard dash wearing nothing but his skivvies. We found out later that someone had put a black snake under his bed covers. I believe that someone was Gene. He was laughing the loudest!

Gene had a great year-round job as a sales representative for an auto parts supplier in Cleveland. His football salary during his last few years with the Browns was "fun" money. Sometimes he'd let his weekly checks from the Browns pile up until Christmas. He didn't need the money, and he loved to taunt Art Modell and his accountant by not cashing the checks.

After football, Gene built a large brick fortress on one hundred acres on the west side of Cleveland. He has a large garden and each summer grows enough vegetables to feed an army. Gene loves food about as much as I do.

BOB GAIN

Bob Gain, the Browns' outstanding defense tackle, tells of how injured players in the 1950s were quickly pulled off the field by teammates to save a time-out. He cited once how he and teammate Don Colo dragged defensive back Warren Lahr off the field by his feet. His head was bouncing along on the ground. They got so much flack about it that the next time they made sure they pulled a player off the field by his shoulders.

Bob was not feeling good one day and was sitting with his doctor. Doc says, what do you eat and drink? Bob says, different foods and one to two shots a day. Doc says, okay, cut down on a few of those foods and only take one shot a day. Bob says, oh, I can't do that Doc. I'm already lying to you.

A lot of people wonder what goes on when there's a big pile of bodies on top of the guy who has the ball and the refs are trying to sort it out, pulling off one player at a time. Everybody under there is wiggling, scratching, clawing, and pulling, trying to get that ball, and if you've got it, you're hanging on for dear life. Nobody stops until the ref says, "Okay, it's so-and-so's ball."

One time, we were playing the Giants and there was a big pile-up. They were fighting underneath for the ball when Bob Gain imitated the ref and said, "Okay, it's the Browns' ball." All the Giants players quit fighting for the ball and our guy holds it up! Bob swears it really was our ball.

One year, some of us started some private financial incentives for teammates who gave special effort during the game. Players would each kick in a few bucks, and we'd award it to some of the big playmakers on Monday following the game. We heard it was illegal after a year or so and never did it again. It was divided up for such things as touchdowns, tackles, interceptions, big blocks, etc. Of course, the defense always wanted something they could sink their teeth into, so three things were added—interceptions, fumbles, and sacks on the quarterback.

We were playing the Giants in New York late in the season, and we had $100 available for sacking their quarterback, Y.A. Tittle. Y.A. may have been old, but he was good, slippery, and smart. If we could get him to just hurry his throws we'd have a better chance to win the game. Well, on this one pass play Tittle threw the ball. About a full two seconds later, while everybody else had started to get up and walk back to the huddle, Bob Gain comes roaring out of nowhere and hits Tittle. WHAM! Tittle's helmet flies off and he's lying there for a minute trying to catch his breath.

Gain goes back to the huddle, and the officials are marking off a roughing the passer penalty against him and we're yelling, "What are you doing, man? What the heck are you doing?" He answered, "All I could think about was that $100!" Thank God, Y.A. was not hurt. We never gave that incentive again.

BATMAN

One of the public relations jobs I had while playing for the Browns was to represent a Euclid hotel called the Charter Haus. On Friday and Monday nights, I would get some of my Browns teammates to speak and make appearances there, to generate more family business in their restaurant. Sometimes had me drive up to the restaurant in a Batmobile. It was a convertible made up like the real Batmobile, and they had me dress like Batman. They would hire a different Browns player each week to dress as Robin. We'd jump out of the car at the hotel and climb a rope ladder two stories high to the roof. Then we'd go through a door from the roof and slide down a pole into the middle of the restaurant. We chased staged villains, especially kids. Anything for a laugh—and a free meal!

BILLY REYNOLDS

Billy Reynolds, Browns halfback, was from Fairmont, West Virginia. His nickname was "Hillbilly." He played his freshman year at Ohio State under Coach Wes Fessler. On weekends he hitchhiked back home. He decided to leave the Buckeyes and go to Pittsburgh his sophomore year. He was an All-American there in 1950, '51, and '52. He was drafted by the Browns in 1953 and offered a salary of $6,000, thirteen payments over the twelve-game season, to sign. Hillbilly demanded a $350 bonus from Paul Brown to purchase a used car. After many arguments, Paul finally gave in to him, but he deducted the bonus from Billy's first game check.

Billy set a kickoff return record in 1954—30 yards per carry. Billy said Paul told him he never wanted to start the offense with the ball on the dirty infield at old Municipal Stadium so he instructed him to bring the ball back at least 30 yards—to get past the dirt. Every Brown teammate of Hillbilly's agreed that if a war ever broke out, you wanted to be in a foxhole with Billy. He was the most loyal Browns player I ever met.

THE MULE MEETS SUPERMAN

The first time I met Jim Brown was in the Cleveland Browns' dressing room. I weighed 218 pounds; he weighed 228. I watched him dress, and he seemed human—put on his pants one leg at a time.

As he dressed he seemed to do everything so nonchalantly. He didn't pull his socks up to the proper height. They seemed wrinkly. He didn't tie his shoestrings tight, didn't tuck his jersey in his pants the whole way, and he didn't seem concerned—no big deal. The equipment man made sure his pads fit properly. Jim Brown was the most muscular man I ever saw. I was impressed! I decided right then I was going to get bigger.

Everything seemed too perfect. I wanted to know this guy's heart. Jim extended his hand and we introduced ourselves to each other. From that moment on, he was "Superman" and I was "the Mule." We had no hang-ups. We connected perfectly. I trust the guy with my life. We built our friendship over many years. Neither of us ever heard the word "quit." We both love challenges.

God molded Jim Brown. He examined His work and said, he looks good. Then He threw the mold away. For the next twenty-nine years, Jim exploited his athletic talents.

Today, Jimmy is known as the greatest athlete to have ever participated in sports. That career includes track, lacrosse, basketball, baseball, and football. He was a college All-American in lacrosse and football and a starter on the basketball team. Drafted by the Boston Celtics, New York Yankees, and Cleveland Browns. Qualified to participate in 1956 Olympics in the decathlon event. Offered $150,000 to become a boxer against Cassius Clay. A low-handicap golfer. Jim Brown is the only athlete to be elected into three Halls of Fame: two in college, one professional.

In the selection of a college, he narrowed it down to Syracuse and Ohio State. There were a lot of rumors that he was to be a Buckeye in 1953. Out of forty-five scholarship offers, he did not have one with the Orangemen.

For statistics freaks: During his nine years as a professional football player, Jimmy played four 12-game seasons and five 14-game seasons. By today's standards, that would equate to having the opportunity to play in twenty-six more season games during his nine seasons. Also, he never had the advantage of playing in indoor, perfect-weather stadiums or on the faster Astro-hard surface fields.

Jimmy will challenge your mind and motives. He tries to develop honest and lasting relationships. He's slow at showing his emotions, but I've seen his eyes well up with real tears when the occasion arises. He has deep feelings for others.

Jimmy was always prepared to face the public on and off the field. He was smart and articulate. His manner was pure, truthful, and subtle. He will deal straight up with any situation. At a book-signing appearance a few years back, my mother was in line to get Jimmy's autograph. She introduced herself, and as he was signing his autograph, Mom said, "Your book about your life was interesting, but the language was pretty strong, especially all those 'F' words." Jimmy said, "Yes, you're right, Mrs. Schafrath. I appreciate your honesty and your opinion. I'm sorry if you found it offensive." He won Mom over—no other apologies were needed.

Jimmy's competitiveness shows off the field, too. Play chess or backgammon with him and you'd better have some big dollar bills and be ready to turn on the midnight oil. I've seen him go all night on many occasions. I once bet him on a game of pool and beat him. He immediately wanted double or nothing. Thirty years later he still remembers.

Jimmy attended every one of my Senate campaign events for sixteen years. I never had to ask him twice. Talk about loyalty.

With Jimmy, there's no BS. Be honest and real, lay it on the table and deal. His philosophy is, "Know the complete facts before you judge somebody." Jim was not afraid to criticize members of his own race, even black leaders, if he thought they deserved it. He's still not afraid.

In a 2002 jailhouse interview with Don Yaeger published in *Sports Illustrated*, Jim took on Michael Jordan, Charles Barkley, and Tiger Woods for failing to do enough to help the black community. He praised them as athletes but said they fail to use their celebrity status and wealth to advance minorities much beyond the area of sports.

He even criticized Martin Luther King, Jr., for heaven's sake! Talk about saying what's on your mind! Who else could get away with that? He said marching and giving speeches won't result in freedom, equality, and justice. Instead, he said, black leaders should be persuading their own people to raise their kids to be educated and responsible for their own actions. He believed that every African American should be working for major changes in our educational system that would help minorities.

At the same time, Jim singled out Bill Belichick, a white coach who was practically run out of Cleveland because he didn't pander to the media, as somebody who did more than many black athletes for the cause of educating blacks and helping rehabilitate gang members. Jim Brown has strong beliefs that he doesn't hold back when he finds an occasion to share them.

IRON MAN

Jim Brown was the sixth pick in the 1957 NFL draft behind Paul Hornung, Jon Arnett, John Brodie, Ron Kramer, and Lenny Dawson. He was 6'2", 230 pounds. Jim combined power with speed, and he could outrun everyone—including opponents and his speedy teammate, Bobby Mitchell, a world-class track sprinter out of the University of Illinois. They'd run races after practice. Everybody would stop what they were doing and watch. All the times I observed them, I can never remember a time when Bobby won. Jimmy was a threat to go all the way from any place on the field.

Pads didn't affect his speed. He could run the same speed with or without them.

Jim Brown was like an iron man. He was a punishing runner! He knew how to use his shoulders and free forearm to ward off defenders. He had tremendous balance because he didn't lift his feet very far off the ground. He ran with sort of a gliding or skating motion. But if somebody tried to tackle him around the legs, he'd lift those knees like pistons and break their hold. He would drag tacklers with him for extra yards. When they finally did bring him down, he would take his time getting back to his feet and move slowly back to the huddle. Then on the next play, he'd explode out of the backfield as fast as ever.

Someone once questioned his blocking ability. Jimmy's response was, "I'm a racehorse, not a plow horse." He did block well when he had to.

Jimmy had the ability to keep his eyes open right up until and through contact. All great athletes have this ability.

Jimmy never let on that he felt pain. He seldom accepted a hand getting off the ground, especially if that hand was attached to an opponent's arm. He wouldn't run out of bounds to avoid a hit, he never left the field for a rest, and only once did I witness him leave the field because of an injury. He missed part of a quarter with a head concussion.

He played some of the 1961 season with a broken toe and sprained wrist. He didn't want anyone to witness him with a weakness. If he had to go to the trainer's room, he'd go before anybody else arrived. After practice, again he'd wait until teammates had gone before getting treatment. He could play well hurt. Every team's defense was designed to stop him.

After Blanton Collier was named head coach, Jim ran more sweeps and quick pitch-outs. He was great at running off the option block on straight-ahead plays. He became a mighty force that propelled us to a championship.

Despite Jimmy's personal excellence, you never saw him high-fiving, dancing, or celebrating on the field. He knew he was doing what he was supposed to be doing. He didn't need to be calling attention to himself. Also, he never taunted opponents. Jim just flipped the ball to the ref after every run as if that was expected of him. Another touchdown—no big deal. That's what he was supposed to do.

Today, you'd think a guy just won a million dollars or it was the end of WWIII if he sacked a quarterback, made a first down, or caught a pass!

The Browns of Jim's day had an inner team pride. He elevated the entire offense. Gary Collins and Paul Warfield became greater ends; they never dropped a pass. Ernie Green and Leroy Kelly were better backs, and Frank Ryan was a better quarterback. The offensive line was a better line. I know our defense even improved.

Our team either led the NFL in rushing or was no less than third throughout the 1960s. Jim Brown both led the league in rushing yardage eight out of nine years and averaged 5.22 yards per carry. Both are NFL records that have not been broken.

Jim Brown, Bobby Mitchell, Leroy Kelly, and Ernie Green all carried the pigskin in the '60s. All four backs were in the Pro Bowl. Three are in the Hall of Fame. The other became an outstanding line coach. We believed and trusted each other. We shared, celebrated, cried, fought, protected, and counted on each other. We knew each other's movements. We could practically read each other's minds. If you made a mistake, you could depend on the guy next to you to cover your backside. You can't get that kind of unified line play by just putting together a bunch of players (regular or all-stars) who are in it for themselves. We were not individuals—we were a team. We were one! We set the standards for all offensive teams in the 1960s.

Our offensive line took its cue from Jimmy in preparing for practice and games. He liked to dress especially lean, and as a result, we did, too. Fewer pads, and the thinner, the better. We wanted to be quick and fast like Jimmy. I'm sure if Jimmy had gone onto the field in a pink jock strap, we would have, too!

In the huddle, the line felt confident with what they could do with Jimmy riding behind us. You could feel the energy and power as we encircled in the huddle. When you looked into his eyes there was a lot of trust and respect. I remember all of us saying at one time or another, "Run it over me, Jimmy." He made you really want to produce. He'd just say, "Okay, Schaf, let's do it!"

I still have a photo of myself blocking against an outstanding defensive end, Lamar Lundy of the Rams. I remember the play because it was fourth and one and I said to our quarterback, Frank Ryan, "Have Jimmy run it over my block. I'll handle my man." Frank called the play. Lundy stood me up, but Jimmy still went flying by, 35 yards, for a touchdown. It wasn't a good block, but Jimmy made me look good.

Before a game, Jim would sit on a stool in the locker room and stare straight ahead. He would be visualizing plays and preparing mentally. I asked him about it one time. He said the plays he made didn't just happen on the field. He would picture the details of each play in full motion beforehand. As he sat on that stool, he'd see himself spinning off a block, using his forearm to stave off a tackler, putting his hand down to keep his balance, giving a defensive back a stiff arm, locking the ball into his hands on a pass. He pictured and anticipated those things, and he was always ready on the field when the occasion called for it.

Jim insisted we work on fundamentals over and over, and he demanded that we practice our offensive drills full go—no going through the motions in a lackadaisical way. Once during practice, he stopped the play and asked for our defensive linebacker to charge at a different angle than he just did. That's what the linebacker would do during the game, and he wanted to see the play like a game situation.

Jimmy, John Wooten (our left guard), and I would get together the nights before ball games and go over our game plan one last time. Actually, Woots and I would go over the game plan. Jimmy mostly watched television and nodded once in awhile when we said, "Is that all right with you?" We wanted to make sure we were all on the same page with our running plays. We'd review our short list of what we called "attitude" plays—the ones we really believed in for crucial situations.

Frank Ryan was good about mixing up the passing and running plays. But sometimes Frank would get to throwing the ball too much, and Jim would say something like, "Slow down, Frank. Let's run a few." When Jimmy's number was called for a few plays, he'd say, "Okay, Frank, you can throw it." I think Frank would have liked to throw the ball on every play, and with Warfield, Collins, Green, and Jimmy catching it, I know why—he had a high completion rate. Frank had five or six outstanding years as our leader.

During these rumbles the line would always agree with Jimmy. We liked to run the ball, so we were always favoring Jimmy when words were exchanged in the huddle. But on the sidelines, there was never much said about it.

After Paul Brown left, Blanton Collier gave our offense a lot of freedom mostly calling our own plays. Dub Jones, our offensive co-ordinator, was excellent to work with. In addition to sweeps, Jim got to run more sprint and option plays. With defenders worried about our great receivers, Jim was even more dangerous. Blanton instituted an option play, which he explained like this: Let the defensive man block himself out of the play. Always take defender the way he wants to go. There is no pre-designated spot a runner must take. He runs towards where the hole should be. If defender does not commit in some direction, blocker must use the head priority finish technique. This allows for the ball carrier to make better decisions. It's a great way to attack a stunting defense. It gives linemen and backs more options. Jim Brown once said, "I would read their blocks and go. I had good peripheral vision. I could pick, and this was ideal for me. Before the option play, I ran mostly as the up man in the I formation. I didn't have a lot of room to play with, [so] the option was a godsend. It was instinctual football, and I averaged about nine yards on that sucker. And if I'd had that option play from day one, my career might have been unbelievable."

As it was, for the first time in years, I was free to roam the entire field and to use all the skills I brought to the game. It was a good year. Liberated by Blanton, with my boys on the line doing some blasting, I was a running fool in 1963. In fourteen games, I rushed for 1,863 yards, averaged 6.4 yards a carry, made 12 touchdowns.

Had games of 162, 232, 175, 123, 144, 223, 154, 179, and 125. Now I was twenty-seven years old. I never ran better in my life.

Today, I think it's ridiculous how coaches rely so much on listing the opponent's play-down tendencies as they prepare for each game. I've seldom seen plays that were successful for one team be just as good for the next. Each team has different strengths depending on their personnel. I told that once to a fellow assistant coach with the Washington Redskins. He thanked me for the suggestion but wanted to keep his job. To me, some of the most exciting challenges of football are to tell your opponent, "We're coming at you. Just try and stop us!"

After Jim Brown retired, Dub Jones balanced the running and passing more, but we lost some of our ability to control the ball in the fourth quarter by either scoring or running out the clock. The philosophy of "run first, pass second" became "run or pass." It was a different theory on how you played the game. Today, most teams pass first, run second!

THE JACKIE ROBINSON OF FOOTBALL

I believe Jimmy felt the unfairness of being treated differently because of his color. He knew he was not inferior to anyone. He never asked for special favors but to be treated equally with the same opportunity as anyone else. He could fight his own battles, choose his own friends, and live where he wanted to.

In all the years I watched Jim at close range, I seldom heard him curse or complain about anything an opponent did to him during a game. When he carried the pigskin, he was the prime target of every defender. Many times, in pile-ups, he would be punched, kicked, bitten, and cursed, but he never fought back or retaliated. That could have been interpreted as a sign of weakness, and if there's anything Jim Brown is not, it's weak!

Jim Brown's self-imposed restraint lasted through his entire career. Each time he carried the football, I believe Jim felt he was carrying the weight of all racial injustices throughout American history on his shoulders. He was making a statement in his own way for all Americans to see. He trained his mind to be immune to pain. Nothing that occurred on the field could hurt him or make him quit.

I only questioned Jimmy one time on the playing field. Early in my career, a screen pass to him was called in the huddle to my side of the field. I was supposed to bump my end, then sprint out and knock down the cornerback. I didn't see why I had to sprint out immediately, because Jim had to wait a couple of seconds before he caught the ball and started to run. He would never catch me. I said as much to him in the huddle. He said, "Just trust me, Schaf. I'll be there."

We ran the play, and I slowed up a little to see when he was coming. Yep, there he was, already on top of me! His cleats were like chainsaws coming up the backs of my legs and then into my back as I went into the turf. I still have the scars. He made his point. From then on, I never questioned Jim Brown's speed or the need to sprint out to the cornerback on a screen. You had to get out there and go full speed. If you slow up, your back has to slow up, and the pursuit is going to catch up and destroy the play.

THE BEST OF ALL RUNNING BACKS

In the early 1960s, we were playing in Dallas against the Cowboys. It was our first trip there and we discovered that blacks and whites couldn't stay together in downtown hotels. All teams would separate for eating and sleeping. We decided we were going to stay together even if it was in tents. We found a low-budget motel near the airport that accepted all of us.

They had an outstanding defense. They had a line of all pros—Jethro Pugh, Bob Lilly, George Andre, Ed "Too Tall" Jones, and Lee Roy Jordan at middle linebacker. Good linebackers and swift defensive backs. We had the ball on their 4-yard line. It was a sweltering 104 degrees. We were behind by four points. There were six seconds left on the clock and we had no more time-outs. A field goal wouldn't do it.

Jim Brown got the call to go off my side. He started off tackle, but didn't see an opening so he took off for the outside—things kept getting worse. About six defensive guys hit him, all bouncing off before he circled back now all the way back to the Dallas twenty. Then he came roaring back toward the goal line. The gun went off and he surged across the goal line with several defenders still hanging on. He had run for about thirty seconds to gain four yards and it seemed everybody on the defense had hit him at least once. Amazing! Jim Brown set a new NFL rushing record and we won.

Afterwards, I was sitting in a whirlpool full of ice water to cool down. I had lost twenty-two pounds. Jimmy came by to shake my hand as he always did, and I noticed he was sucking on an ice cube.

On the field, Jim Brown was like a man obsessed. I've never seen a runner like him and no one ever will. When the chips were down, we all wanted him to carry the ball. And he wanted the ball. I don't think I'll get many arguments about that. He was the best athletic to ever play sports. Jim Thorpe was a close second. Jackie Robinson, third. That's the way I rated them during the days when mostly white athletics prevailed.

Jim Brown had no use for the hype or self-promotion that's so prevalent in sports today. But he does have a sense of his place in the history of professional football. In the mid-1990s, he was addressing a money management club in Cleveland. During the question and answer period, someone asked, "Mr. Brown, who in your opinion is the greatest back of all time? Is it O. J. Simpson, Franco Harris, Walter Payton, Barry Sanders, Gale Sayers or yourself?"

Jim listened to the question, thought for a moment and gave this answer. "All of them were great backs", he said. "They all had different running styles, offensive lines, and played in different times."

Then lowering his voice he said, "Let me set the stage. The ball is on the opponent's one-yard line, you're four points behind, no time outs left, two seconds on the clock and it's fourth down. I'd give the ball to Jim Brown!"

The crowd roared its approval.

JIM BROWN'S RETIREMENT

Much has been said about Jimmy's sudden retirement in 1966, but I'd like to shed a little light on it from a teammate's standpoint. When we came to training camp at Hiram, we had come off a great year. I was captain, and it was to be the first season of the Super Bowl.

We were told Jimmy would be a few days late reporting, maybe a week, but not to be concerned. He was finishing a film in England, and there were some delays due to the weather. The film was *The Dirty Dozen* and he had one of the lead roles. We blocked out everything about Jimmy reporting late and were working hard at practice with one goal—to win our division and then, the first Super Bowl!

Toward the end of that week, rumors started quickly circulating that Jimmy had been given notice by team owner Art Modell—either get back with the team or be fined $100 a day; even worse, he could permanently retire from the team. These words sounded scary. Why was Jimmy being threatened and backed into a corner? It was the wrong thing to do. Then at the end of the week, the bomb hit. He finished the movie and his football career at the same time. I suddenly felt sick to my stomach.

I first talked to Coach Collier about it, then Jimmy's close friend John Wooten. Was there anything we could do to change his mind? Both said, "No." I called Jimmy. He was upbeat about it—said it was time to move on and reassured me we'd be okay with Leroy and Ernie. He was going to pursue new challenges. Not taking anything away from Leroy or Ernie (their records stand for themselves), they were both outstanding backs, leaders, and winners. But losing Jimmy? He was the greatest back ever. He was our heart and soul! He was the one person who had lifted our team above winners to a championship level.

Something drastic had to have happened to cause Jim Brown to suddenly walk without a good-bye. Jimmy loved to win more than anyone I ever knew. He was not all wrapped up in statistics. I believe after we won the World Championship game in '64 he was ready to move on to other personal challenges. Losing the championship game in '65 sealed his determination to pursue a movie career and leave football. Art Modell's threat just helped confirm it.

Jim and I have talked about the exorbitant salaries today's players make. He says, "Schaf, I never thought about money. The sport offered a lot of satisfying personal challenges. I loved the accomplishments we had as a team—it was fun and rewarding and we were champions. Not everyone has an opportunity to reach that plateau. It's time to move on."

THE BROWNS' AMAZING RUNNING BACKS

With Leroy Kelly and Ernie Green, our running game never skipped a beat. They really complimented each other even though we fell into a more predictable running pattern. Kelly ran mostly right, Ernie mostly left. It didn't seem to matter which way they ran—both made yards. Mentally, we were all set for Jimmy to return in 1966 for his last season, but when he retired, Leroy Kelly moved in. The rest is history. Leroy led the NFL in rushing two seasons, and he's in the Hall of Fame, too. But nobody is Jim Brown. He was a force all on his own. The back that helped put both Jimmy and Leroy into the Hall of Fame was Ernie Green. Ernie is listed number six on the Browns' all-time yardage gainer list with 3,200 and an average 4.8 per carry. He compiled these stats while in the same backfield with two Hall of Famers and perennial NFL rushing leaders. He led the team in touchdowns one season.

I'm convinced that with Jimmy, the Browns would have been a Super Bowl winner, too. He retired prematurely. Otherwise, we would have had the three best backs in football—Brown, Kelly, and Green. Together, they would have been something special.

Jimmy still had not peaked when he retired. He was getting better each year. His best was 1965, and he still loved to play and win. With him, the entire offense played at a higher level.

Leroy Kelly loved contact and was a great special teams player! He was always one of the first players to be downfield to make the tackles. He returned punts and kickoffs. On offense he showed he was a great competitor and could do it all. He ran low and hard—difficult to knock off his feet, had great balance and an exceptionally quick start. A good muddy field runner. Seemed to get stronger as the game went along. He never tired. A dependable leader by example.

Ernie Green was an underrated player. He could do it all—very dependable both running and catching. The best blocker of the three, he could have also played tight end if Jimmy and Leroy had been in backfield at the same time. He was the best positive to come from the closing chapter of Paul Brown. Until he retired, Ernie was the glue that held us all together. People often talk about what it would have been like with Ernie Davis, but with Ernie Green in the backfield, the team became the best running team ever.

Another thing, or at least a good second guess: We should never have traded Bobby Mitchell in 1962. He should have been moved to a receiver position. With him, we would have had three Hall of Fame-caliber receivers—Warfield, Collins, and Mitchell. Warfield and Mitchell are in the Hall of Fame. Collins should be, too. I'd love to have seen teams try to cover them with Jimmy, Kelly, and Green in the backfield.

CHARLEY SCALES

Charley entered the huddle late during a game in the early 1960s. A pass play was called. Quarterback fumbled the ball and Charley picked it up, Rather than run, he thought he'd finish the pass play. He threw it. He completed it, but to an opposing team player.

On the sidelines Coach Brown asked, "How'd that happen?" Charley said, "I'm sorry, I made a mistake." Paul Brown said, "Son, forget it. I promise you, you'll NEVER make that mistake again!"

JIM NINOWSKI

Quarterback Jim Ninowski was one of my favorites. He had a great personality and a lot of ability, but he never seemed to get a break. Every team needs a Jim Ninowski. He kept us loose, but never so loose as the day we were playing the Steelers in an exhibition game at the Akron Rubber Bowl. I've never seen anything like this, before or since.

On our first offensive series we linemen came out of the huddle, went to the line, and got into our three point stances. Ninowski suddenly forgot where he was and he put his hands under the left guard instead of the center and started to call the cadence. John Wooten, the guard, yelled at him, "Get away!" Ninowski backed up and gathered himself for a second all the time trying to look calm and confident. But to him, all our butts looked the same. He confidently swaggered back up to the line, but he went the wrong way again and this time he put his hands under me at left tackle. Now I shouted, "Get out of here!" The officials started laughing along with the whole Steelers defense, and Ninowski had to call a time out so we could regroup.

MONTE CLARK'S NIGHTMARE

We're playing an exhibition game against the Los Angeles Rams in their Coliseum. Our offense is up against the "Fearsome Foursome"—every one of their defensive lineman was an All-Pro. Their biggest name, Deacon Jones, was not playing in this game, though. He was holding out for more money on his contract. No right tackle looked forward to battling the Deacon—you had to be well prepared and performing at the top of your game. In the dressing room our right tackle, Monte Clark, was the only lineman not nervous. He was playing against a rookie. Everyone else knew they had their hands full.

The game was well in our favor in the first half and everyone was feeling pretty good. One more quarter and all regulars could call it a day, as our second teamers and tryouts were scheduled to play the rest.

We received the second half kickoff, and while our offense started to gather in the huddle, there's a loud, terrible groan. It's Monte Clark, and he's really in pain. "Ohhh, ohhh—Nooo! nooo!"

he's crying louder. Frank Ryan, our quarterback, says, "Monte are you alright? Should I call time out?" Monte's still groaning, but pointing to the sidelines. Then a tremendous roar goes up from the crowd. It's Deacon Jones, live in uniform, trotting out onto the field. He suddenly decided to play the second half without a contract. Monte spotted him coming out of the dressing room before anyone else. He was not prepared to face him. We all laughed in the huddle. Monte didn't think it was funny.

JOE "TURKEY" JONES

Each year when the final Browns roster was decided and the regular season began, the veterans would start leaking out the message: Free Turkeys for everyone at Thanksgiving time. Usually two rookies would be volunteered to pick up all the veterans' turkeys on Wednesday of Thanksgiving week right after practice. A signup sheet was posted on a bulletin board for everyone to order their turkeys. A diagram with directions to the turkey farm was written on the backside.

Guys would sign up weeks ahead of time. Some would add names of cousins, girlfriends, and grandparents. But the whole thing was a lark. There was no such address, and no free turkeys. No rookie ever admitted they couldn't find the turkey farm, though. They were always too embarrassed to admit they had been tricked. But it was good for a lot of laughs and ribbing the next day.

One year Joe Jones, a rookie, took the bait hook, line, and sinker. Joe was relentless in his search for the turkey farm. He wouldn't give up. He borrowed a pickup truck, took the list and directions, and looked for at least four hours. He called at least a dozen veterans and coaches for help with the problems he was having. Everyone told him to try another road and keep looking for a big sign. One veteran finally told him it was all a joke to just go on home. But Joe wouldn't believe him—he kept looking. A farmer had the police and sheriff department stop and question him. The result, for the rest of his career and to this day, all former teammates know Joe as "Turkey" Jones.

ON THE LINE

One day we were playing the Giants in New York. My opponent was Andy Robustelli. Today, he is a Hall of Famer. I'm sure he's there because of a lot of my performances against him. It was the middle of the second quarter, and I was battling him the best I could. The crowd was extremely noisy, and on one particular play I could not hear the quarterback's starting count in the huddle. One thing you do need to know when you're blocking a great end is the starting count so at least you have a chance to get off the ball quicker than he does.

The whole way to the line of scrimmage I was asking John Wooten, "Woots, what's the count? Woots, what's the count?" He tried to whisper it a couple of times, but I couldn't hear him. He was not about to yell out loud because he didn't want his own defensive man, Rosey Grier, to hear him. When we got down in our stance, out of desperation I yelled out, "Woots, what's the count?" Robustelli yelled back, "On two, stupid!" I wondered, how the heck does he know that? On two the ball was snapped. After the play was over, I asked Andy how he knew. He said, "I just assumed it would be since the first twenty plays were!" Needless to say, our quarterback mixed up the starting count from then on.

ART MODELL AND PAUL BROWN: THE END OF A DYNASTY

Two icons from different worlds had come together in 1961: Art Modell and Paul Brown.

During Modell's second year as owner, there were a lot of rumors that he and Paul Brown weren't getting along very well—front office problems. Modell wanted to be involved in day-to-day operations as well as marketing and advertising. He shadowed Paul's every move every day. A more noticeable thing occurred just before our regular season started in 1962. We had just played the 49ers and were staying in the San Francisco area for a week practicing before going to Los Angeles to play the Rams. We were at the San

Francisco airport and everyone was going into a lounge because our plane was an hour late. Art was there buying everyone beer. He said, "The drinks are on me." Paul Brown came down the hall, saw us, and went berserk! "Out of here! Out of here! My players can't drink in public." Art was apologetic and did not say another word.

Prior to one game, Art gave the team a pep talk.

Paul approached Art and told him that he'd "appreciate it if he stayed out of the locker room before games. This is private, between myself and the players. You don't belong here." Another thing that had Art boiling was Paul trading future Hall of Famer Bobby Mitchell without consulting with him before the 1962 draft. Paul traded Bobby to the Redskins for their first-round pick. Paul wanted All-American Ernie Davis.

I don't think Art was trying to undermine Paul. My interpretation of it was they both thought they owned the team and did not want to relinquish control. Art, the real owner, wanted to know everything about his new investment and spontaneously did things without asking questions. He had no other occupation. He was always at the practice field, in the locker room, and on the sidelines. He breathed and absorbed football 24/7/365. He never took a moment off. When not with the team, Art was attending team-related functions or entertaining clients at The Theatrical, the popular downtown bar and restaurant.

Paul always seemed annoyed and uncomfortable by it all. He thought Art should stay out of the day-to-day hands-on football activities. He was also general manager and always had full control over players. I don't think the difficulties between Jimmy Brown and Paul Brown had much of anything to do with Paul being fired.

Equally shocking was that within three short years, Art had fired the greatest coach ever and gave the greatest running back ever an ultimatum to play or retire. The fans still stayed behind Art through good and bad times for the next thirty-four years.

This new thirty-six-year-old owner was a young cigarette-smoking, beer drinking, New York marketing executive who was still living at home with his mother. He saw an opportunity to own the best team in football and jumped in with both feet and started to run. Art was so green at his new position that he got lost the first day trying to find our training camp at Hiram College. Isolated in the Ohio hills, it wasn't easy to find.

Paul and Art butted heads from the start. Neither was willing to give an inch. It was a very tense two years. Everything came to an abrupt end with all guns blazing when Art fired Paul.

Paul was viewed successful at winning football games. Fans would support you if you were a winner. And Paul was the best in the world at winning. He did not care about Art Modell's money-making ideas. In fact, I think he was annoyed at Art's scheduling double-headers—four years of playing back-to-back games.

Later on, Art was confident fans would buy into all his marketing and merchandising hype—and they did. He was successful with everything he tried. Besides double-headers, he welcomed the AFL into the NFL arena through a Super Bowl game. He started Monday night football, fireworks at games, entertainment before and after games. He helped negotiate a gigantic merchandising contract for all players and teams.

Football exploded when Art helped sign large TV contracts for all teams to share. Besides paying customers, millions of Americans and Canadians suddenly got 50-yard-line seats via television. NFL games that were formally regional. Now, because of national TV, football was challenging baseball as America's pastime sport. In 1964, it only took the Browns seven games to draw more fans than the Cleveland Indians did in eighty-one games. In 1946, it was $10,000 per team via TV contracts. In 1964, $10,000,000 per team via TV contracts. In 2005, $80,000,000 per team via TV contracts. Art recommended all stadiums be rebuilt to serve fans with comfortable seats and huge instant-replay scoreboards.

In any event, I loved both Paul and Art.

I did not see or talk to Coach Brown until maybe eight to ten years after he was fired. The Browns were playing an exhibition game against the Bengals at Fawcett Stadium in Canton. Before the game I said, "Hi, Coach." We shook hands and he said, "Keep up the good work, Schaf. You're still one of my boys." Most of his boys, including me, attended his funeral in Massillon some years later.

I don't even want to touch the matter of Art moving the team. But all athletes playing today should kiss Art's picture for the great salary opportunities they enjoy.

My sister Kathleen (I affectionately called her Yuk) and I taking a bath after a hard day's work on the farm.

Me, Mom, and Kathleen after church in our front yard during the early 1940s. You can see our classic Chevys in the background.

The 150-year-old farmhouse where I was raised and my parents lived until they passed away. Kathleen is on the left with my brother Larry peaking out of the bottom of the frame.

Until I was approximately ten years old, we farmed like the Amish. We had four horses and two mules. Here my father and I are getting ready to use real horse power to haul manure.

This is the whole family in my 1955 high school graduation photo right before I left for Ohio State. (Left to Right) Front Row: Kathleen, Ed, Mike, Bernard, Larry, Back Row: Me, Mom, and Dad.

Back in the 1940s I used to pitch in a hot-stove league. I would practice pitching against the side of our barn everyday. Sometimes I would pretend I was on the 1948 Indians.

I never saw a football game until I played in one. My football career began in high school with the Wooster Generals. I played fullback and middle linebacker all four years.

My father helped me train calves to show at the Wayne County Fair. Heifers like this one would act just fine until they were in front of the judges, then they forgot all training.

My first wife, Bonnie, and I met in high school. Here we are in 1957, the summer before we got married, taking a break from work on the farm.

Legendary Ohio State coach Woody Hayes (center) recruited me during my junior and senior years in high school. In 1958 Woody picked Frank Kremblas (right) and me to be co-captains of the football team.

The last play of the 1958 OSU-Michigan game. The Wolverines were on our goal line with a minute left. I (#71) made the tackle that caused Michigan to fumble. (Note the ball at lower right.) We won, 20-14.

The great 1960s Browns offensive line (left to right): Monte Clark, Gene Hickerson, John Morrow, John Wooton, and me. We loved to run, and run we did. We led the league in rushing and helped three offensive backs and one end rush into the Hall of Fame.

I always overestimated my opponents' physical abilities. But as good as they were, I was going to find some way to get my job done. Here I am, suiting up for another battle.

The last World Championship Game took place at Municipal Stadium in 1964 against the Baltimore Colts. Here, I (#77) block a Colts defensive back for Jim Brown (#32). We shut out Baltimore, 27-0.

I was the first Browns player to lift weights. In this picture I weighed 270, up from 215 my rookie season. My two-year-old son Jeff is giving me a little extra help.

In 1978 I posed as Victor the Bear at the Cleveland Sports Show. Attendees lined up with money in hand to wrestle me. My son Gerrit (age 3) would lead me out into the ring.

This may not have been my usual breakfast, but I'm known for having a ferocious appetite. In a bid to gain weight, I entered eating contests all over. I never lost.

In 1969, I volunteered to go to Vietnam on a USO tour. Nothing compares with the experience of visiting our military people during that war. They are the real heroes.

My mother and father attended when I was sworn into the Ohio Senate on July 3, 1985 by the Honorable Michael R. McKinley, the Director of the Ashland Court of Common Pleas.

In 2003 I was inducted into the Cleveland Browns Legends Club. Joe DeLamielleure, Bob Gain, and Hanford Dixon joined me during the halftime ceremony.

My family (left to right, from top): Mom and Dad Schafrath, Judy Grimm, Bonnie Kubin
Jeff Denim, Renée Raper, Ty Schafrath,
Isaac Schafrath, Gerrit Schafrath, Bruin Schafrath, Heidi Hoffmann.

CHAPTER SIX

A NEW ERA

CHANGING OF THE GUARD

After Blanton Collier was picked for the Browns' head coaching job, we heard rumors that Paul didn't want him to accept the position. Blanton had very loyal heart, and he felt uncomfortable succeeded his friend as the second head coach of the Cleveland Browns. Paul did have him worrying whether or not to accept the job. Blanton and I both lived in Aurora, and we talked about it at his home when we studied game films together. Blanton did a great job pulling everybody together and moving on. In his nine seasons as head coach, he always had a winning team, and we were always in some type of play-off game. He was very approachable and easy to talk to. He had a great passion to win. He'd talk football with your great-grandmother, the Pope, or anyone else who would listen. He never stopped. If he liked someone, he referred to them as "good people."

Blanton Collier kept the same coaches and the same players. He did bring in a couple more good offensive warriors in 1963: Monte Clark, John Brown, and a good young defensive tackle named Jim Kanicki. We were all maturing together both mentally and physically. But there was a sudden attitude change, too. We believed in each other, and we believed we could win! In 1963 we finished 10-4. We all were upset—we felt we should have won our division. Instead, we were playing in the runner-up "Nothing Bowl" in Miami against the Green Bay Packers.

After that season I believe the team wanted to prove to everyone that we could win without Paul Brown, and Blanton was the perfect coach to get us to do it. He encouraged players with positive suggestions. Our commitment to winning under Blanton in 1964 was at an all-time high. A lot of people compared our offense to Green Bay's during the '60s. As great as the Packers were, we still averaged close to one yard more per carry. I give all the credit to Coach Collier. He taught the blocking techniques in such a way that you could picture yourself doing everything exactly as he said. Hickerson, Wooten, Clark, Morrow, and I loved to run, and run we did. In five of Blanton's eight years we led the league in rushing and helped two backs rush into the Hall of Fame.

BLANTON COLLIER'S SECOND YEAR

In 1964, we picked up two future Hall of Famers, Paul Warfield and Leroy Kelly, and a few other good players in the draft. Also, we obtained an experienced leader, Dick Modzelewski, defensive tackle from the New York Giants. We all worked hard in the off-season preparing, so we were in great shape for the first day of training camp. When training camp opened in 1964, I knew we were capable of winning it all. That's all we talked about. We were obsessed with winning. We thought about it, practiced, and played like it. That was a fun year—for us and for the fans. A year to remember.

We all immediately advanced to a higher level. Yeah, maybe we had something to prove when Paul left. There was an attitude change, and it made the transition look good. We were committed and came out of the gates running. We were ready to win. We *expected* to win! We got very emotional with Blanton. We had developed a passion and true desire to win.

Blanton Collier and all the assistant coaches stayed together through most of the 1960s. Blanton had been our offensive coordinator. He was just starting to get it through our linemen's heads how to option block, which we also called "sprint blocking." We had a four-step process to follow when we fired off the ball—hit, drive, climb, and finish. It developed into something exciting, especially since you could get more than one block if you hustled. Blanton lived and breathed head priority. He maintained it was key to our successful running game. I could add that having runners like Jim Brown, Leroy Kelly, and Ernie Green helped, too.

THE GEORGE THEORY

Another thing Blanton Collier emphasized was, "Don't let George do it; you do it!" The George Theory was that great athletes always make the great plays. But any player can make a big play if you try hard enough. He referred to making great plays as "George plays." Blanton would say, "Don't just let the great players do it. You be George! You do it! Each of you can be George if you have the desire and want it bad enough. Enough Georges and we'll be champions!" My attitude was always, "I'm going to be George and make a big block. I'll hustle downfield on every play. I'll be the one to spring the back loose. Make one block and hustle to make another one on the same play." All our offensive team shared this attitude.

Jimmy, Leroy, or Ernie would be still running after getting through the line of scrimmage, and we all discovered that after doing our initial job, we could sometimes make another block if we hustled. Before that, you did your four-step job at the point of attack, then got up and watched the play until it finished. Trot back to the huddle and say, "Let's go again!" Our play was starting to become a little more advanced. It evolved into a different game. Having an experienced line really helped.

That's what Jimmy liked about our line. Everyone had that same running attitude. It kind of rubbed off. Everybody was always hustling and throwing at someone. You weren't satisfied with just blocking one person. You kept going, trying to get another hit, all the way to the goal line.

One other Blanton philosophy played a major role in the 1964 success. Blanton was a great believer in psycho-cybernetics. Just sit down and picture every phase of your block, or running at, around, or through a defense or catching a pass, pulling in the ball then running with it. Visualize every move, prepare in detail for every game. Blanton taught this well, and meditation worked miracles for some of our players. More about this later.

A LINE OF WARRIORS:
MY OFFENSIVE LINE TEAMMATES, 1959–1971

Left Guard, no. 64, Jim Ray Smith (Texas)—Fast and strong. Made All Pro every year he played for the Browns (1957–62). Best lineman I ever played with except for Jim Parker at Ohio State. He was traded to Dallas after '62 so he could be closer to his family and business. Retired early in career. Pro Bowl—five times.

Left Guard, no. 60, John Wooten (Colorado)—Drafted by Cleveland the same year I was, 1958. He was a leader who commanded a lot of respect. Was messenger guard with Hickerson for the first two seasons. The liaison between coaches, line, backs, and quarterback. Became full-time starter in '62. Blocked for three Hall of Fame backs (Mitchell, Brown, and Kelly). Retired early in career. Pro Bowl several times.

Center, no. 56, John Morrow (Michigan)—Tough as a bull. He was the guy you wanted to protect your backside. Played one series with a broken tibia bone sticking out of his sock until we scored. Always had a dripping nose. Some of it was always hanging in his face mask bars. We all accepted this behavior knowing he was a Michigan graduate. Captain of line calls. Nothing rattled him. He could be going over Niagara Falls in a canoe and he'd be yawning. Named All Pro several times.

Right Guard, no. 66, Gene Hickerson (Ole Miss)—Our Hall of Famer. Was quick, strong, and had great balance. Excelled on sweeps and trap-blocking. A man of few words. Messenger guard 1958–60. Broke leg in 1961. Starter 1962–73; All Pro six times. Blocked for three Hall of Fame backs (Mitchell, Brown, Kelly).

Right Tackle, no. 74, Mike McCormick (Kansas)—Team captain. Had good balance, quick feet. Was an outstanding leader. Pro Bowl five times. Played hurt his last season. Elected to Hall of Fame. Played 1953–62. Won two championship rings. Hall or Famer. Pro Bowl several times.

Right Tackle, no. 73, Monte Clark (University of Southern California)—Traded to Cleveland 1963. A converted defensive tackle.

Was strong and tough. A great battler. Constantly in a fistfight. Excellent downfield blocker. Retired after 1969 to become offensive line coach at Miami. Has the only perfect NFL team record, 17-0. Later became head coach of San Francisco 49ers and the Detroit Lions.

Right Tackle, no. 70, John Brown (Syracuse)—Back up to Clark and me. Had good balance, good speed, a great team player. Lacked size to take the pounding of being a regular, but made up for it with a winning heart.

Tight End, no. 83, Johnny Brewer (Ole Miss)—He was big, lean, and mean. He was the same size as the offensive linemen. Tremendous blocker, especially down on ends and hooking line backers. His hook blocks got our sweeps going. Made a lot of important catches. All Pro.

Lou Groza, no. 76 (Ohio State)—Played 21 seasons, all with the Browns. Great tackle, great kicker, great leader. All Pro. Hall of Famer. Deceased.

Any one of my offensive teammates had the talent and ability to be in the Hall of Fame, especially if we let them be the focal point of our team and selfishly do their own thing. But no one is there.

Together at one time or another we blocked against sixteen Hall of Fame defensive linemen, thirteen Hall of Fame middle line backers, and thirteen Hall of Fame defensive backs while leading three backs and one end into the Hall of Fame.

THE MENTAL ADVANTAGE

In *Psycho-Cybernetics*, Dr. Maxwell Maltz showed that within a week, those who visualized their assignments every day in a clear and vivid manner performed in actual tests at about the same level as those who physically practiced the same skills each day. Wow, what tremendous implications for all sports, especially football!

You can only spend so much time hitting, tackling, scrimmaging, catching, and running, but you can spend so much more time visualizing the details of playing your position. And of course, you won't experience any physical pain or damage.

Each "mental rep" requires you to picture the specific details of your position on each play until it becomes a habit. Thus, when you hit the field, you will have already been successful hundreds of times. You win on every play. A lot of people misunderstand this visualizing concept and call it "voodooism" or "hypnotism."

Coach Collier introduced me and many of my Browns teammates to this mental-advantage concept in the early 1960s. Monte Clark and I immediately adopted this "picture concept" to go along with our normal on the field game practices. It became part of our daily game preparation. It did for others, too.

Each evening and each morning, as faithful as reading the Bible, we'd take twenty minutes, find a quiet place to relax (preferably with some soft music playing), close our eyes, and picture ourselves performing one-on-one against our opponent. We'd go through each run, each pass, using perfect techniques. Dominating our man on runs and fighting his every move. Protecting our quarterback on passes. Always performing at a high level of intensity.

I found that I was extremely focused and more confident come game day when I had prepared all week using the mental advantage over and above my regular on-field physical work.

I'm talking about visualizing every little detail of every play. How I stood in the huddle listening to the quarterback call the play. Jogging to the line of scrimmage. Getting into my stance. Seeing the color of the opponent's jersey. Keeping my eyes open and focused on the numbers of my target, smoking out of my stance, exploding into my block, always keeping my head priority, climbing him with my feet, digging to gain control. Walling and finishing him as my back sprints by for a big gain. Then, hustling my butt off, sprinting downfield to try and make another block. On a trap play stepping quickly with my lead foot in the direction I was pulling. Running low and taking a good inside-out angle to gain depth on the man I was to trap. Getting into a linebacker numbers quickly, head up; delivering a big hit with both fists, making sure to keep head priority until finish as the back makes his cut off my block.

I wanted my opponent to know that if he was waiting for me to let up during our battle, that was not going to happen.

You can visualize yourself working through obstacles like heat, cold, fatigue, hurts, away-game hostile crowds and make everything an advantage for you.

I always overestimated my opponents' physical abilities. But as good as they were, I was going to find some way to get my job done. If it became an all-out nasty fistfight, I was going to prevail. I would never give up; I would never quit. I wanted it more than he did!

Visualization can help anyone to play at a higher level. Many athletes have used the mental advantage. They just seldom share this edge with others. I already mentioned two teammates, Jim Brown and Monte Clark. For me, this type of concentration and picturing gave better results than I had ever experienced before.

To keep improving faster, never be completely satisfied that you played your best. Always feel you can do better. If this becomes your daily attitude, you can be pretty darn sure something good is going to happen for you and your teammates. The ladder to becoming a champion also requires discipline in every part of your life. Any person who does not know how to prepare is mainly dependent on hoping and wishing. I'm convinced it played a big part in winning the world championship in 1964.

WINNING DISCIPLINE, MY WAY

First, physical discipline. Get plenty of rest, treat all ailments, stretch properly before and after workouts. Don't let up on a play until after whistle blows. Eat balanced meals. Take plenty of water, fruits, and vegetables. Maintain a good weight for your position. Work hard with a daily plan to improve your strength, flexibility, speed, quickness, and stamina. Be prepared to give 100 percent for sixty minutes every time you are on the field.

Second, mental and psychological discipline. Mental advantage helps you improve your performance to the point where you can stretch to try and approach your full potential. The more repetitions you do, the quicker they will become a habit. Know your game backwards and forwards. Picture your techniques and assignments over and over each day. Study your opponent on film. Know his strengths and weaknesses. Anticipate the little things that could and will happen and picture yourself reacting to them. A good way to gain additional mental reps on the practice field is to know what play is called when it's your alternate's turn. Think through all the details of the play and learn from what you're watching. Great performances don't happen automatically; they're part of your game preparation. Become an expert at your position.

Third, spiritual discipline. Your heart and attitude are strong sources of power. A daily spiritual plan is an individual responsibility. If you don't have your own personal plan and are doing only what the coaches require, then you are not even scratching the surface of your potential. Keeping the Lord number one in your life is a tremendous advantage for being an unselfish winning-team player. Don't try to be someone you're not.

I have heard a lot of players say, "I have done everything the coaches have asked of me." Well, unless your personal preparation plan is similar to what I have described above, and you already use a similar, better, more encompassing plan, then don't kid yourself. You're not doing all you can to be a champion.

Fourth, team discipline. Team players play with a singleness of purpose. They sacrifice personal goals and are happy for teammates' success. The importance and the need to produce vivid mental pictures of your performance is a responsibility that both players and coaches need to share in all their dealings together, whether on the field, watching films, at the blackboard, or in conversation. All parties must be striving to achieve the same results on every play.

1964 WORLD CHAMPIONS: A TEAM OF UNSELFISH PLAYERS WHO CARED ABOUT ONE ANOTHER

In 1964, we were getting ready for our showdown with the Baltimore Colts in what was then called the world championship. The winner of the NFL Eastern Conference played the winner of the Western Conference. It would be two more years before they changed the name to the Super Bowl, Commissioner Pete Rozell's brilliant idea!

Everyone picked us to lose. *Sports Illustrated* writers called the Eastern Conference teams a joke. Critics were saying that three teams from the west were better than the east's best. That the Baltimore Colts had won the world title in October when they beat Green Bay. That our zone defense would be torn apart by Baltimore receivers, we had no pass rush, and only blitzed occasionally.

We were at practice on Tuesday in a team meeting. Blanton Collier was looking us over; then, as he spoke, everything turned quiet. "Men," he said, "we are going to win." We had a lot of confidence in Blanton. He presented a simple game plan for the offense that demanded good execution, a positive attitude, and total commitment.

In retrospect, I think we had that game won on Tuesday. I know I felt real good. When you feel good on Tuesday of game week, it's a good sign. Most games are won or lost early in the week. That's when you get mentally prepared. It's too late to get hyped up and ready on game day. There are too many distractions. You may be talking to me on game day, but I don't hear what you're saying. I'm already blocking. I'm protecting the passer. I got that from Jimmy. He'd be in the locker room before a game. We'd ask, "Why are you just sitting there staring into space?" He'd say, "I'm picturing myself running."

Gary Collins was riding home with me from practice that Tuesday when I said, "What do you think, Futz?"

"We're gonna win by two touchdowns," he replied.

"I'll take one point!" I said, less confidently.

"No, I'm serious, Schaf. Their defensive backs can't stop both Paul [Warfield] and me. One of us will always be open. Just make sure your line gives Frank [Ryan] time to throw. We'll catch 'em."

Of course I knew Futz always wanted the ball. What good end doesn't? He'd always say, "Just throw me the damn ball; I'm open." Gary seldom, if ever, dropped a pass. He had great hands. If he could touch it, he would catch it. He could do it all.

Collins and Warfield were both great ends. Complete players. They ran perfect patterns for Ryan to throw to. Warfield was probably the best blocking receiver in the NFL. He was explosive and got into you quick. He once put Doug Atkins on his back. Of course, he hit Doug from the blindside, but Atkins was six foot six and 290 pounds!

In the meantime, our offensive line and Jim Brown were just as confident about our running game. Our halfback, Ernie Green, was a great all-around player. Most important, he was an outstanding blocker! Also, we had a great blocking tight end in Johnny Brewer. He was like having a third tackle. He could really stand ends and linebackers up and hook them to get our sweeps started. Our concern was whether our defense could stop the Colts' great Johnny Unitas and Lenny Moore. Our defense had to have a great game. Possibly whoever scored last would win.

I had a Volkswagen Bug, and Collins and I rode to practice in it each day. The windows were always frozen because the defroster did not work well, if at all. Gary would be hanging out of the window every five minutes, wiping the windshield so we could see. The slush and mist from snow, salt, and dirt sometimes made driving the Bug nearly impossible. Sometimes we took to the sidewalks to pass traffic, but we had no accidents.

Since Gary was so confident we were going to win, I arranged for a team party after the game at a downtown hotel. I arranged for a band, too, so that we could really celebrate. The day before the game, after we loosened up at the stadium for our dress rehearsal, I said good-bye to Bonnie and the kids and checked into the team hotel early to be by myself and relax. But then I got restless. It was still early afternoon, so I decided to walk to a local movie theater across the street and catch a film. The usher escorted me to a seat (the old-fashioned way) with his flashlight. I thanked him and sat down to enjoy the film. I thought it was a little odd having an usher since I could not see another person in the theater. In a few moments here comes the light again; the usher is escorting another guy to a seat right beside me. I look up and it is Ordell Brasse, my opponent for tomorrow's game! We both quickly found seats as far from each other as possible.

Talk about irony! Brasse had been very much on my mind since midweek, when Hank Critchfield called to say, "Hate to put any pressure on you, Schaf, but I just heard from a good friend of mine in Baltimore. He said that your match-up with Brasse is the key to the outcome of the game."

No pressure there! Thanks, Hank, for the great news.

I hardly slept at all that night. I kept practicing my positive mental reps, but I was constantly interrupted with visions of no. 81 sprinting past me as my feet are frozen to the ground. I went to church early game day and said a lot of short prayers, promising the Lord how good I'd be if He allowed me to have a good game and for us to win.

It was a cold day—and windy! I ate a breakfast of steak and eggs and left early for the stadium with Gene Hickerson. Woody Hayes always said, "Cold is only in your mind." This day was a good day to test his theory. I had no thoughts about anything but Brasse.

The stadium was still pretty empty, the wind was blowing, and the temperature was near freezing. It was Browns weather—perfect for us, bad for Baltimore!

My Uncle Bill met me on the field. I had asked him to come and take some pictures, posing as a newspaper photographer from Wooster. He had no trouble getting on the field with me. I asked him something stupid, like whether he had some film in the camera. I found out later that because he was so nervous, he took most of the pictures with the lens cap still on the camera. I was pretty relaxed, as I did a lot of stretching. The stadium was starting to fill up. I kept watching for my family to appear in the stands. I was oblivious to the cold.

When I first got to the dressing room I went to the bathroom, the first of about two dozen times. I got my ankles taped. All players had to have their ankles taped. I guess it was kind of a preventive-injury unwritten rule. We had to do this in college, too. Next, I got my hands and wrists taped. I always cut some rubber padding out to fit the top of my hands before applying the tape. It gave me a lot of strong support when I hit pads or helmets. Most offensive linemen did this. If you were playing at home, you painted the tape white. This was because we wore white jerseys at home games. It would be harder for officials to see you holding if you grabbed someone. If you played an away game, you painted the tape dark. You had to use every advantage. Next, I got a twenty-minute massage on my neck and shoulders. That felt great, but I was starting to get a little concerned. By now I should be more psyched up for the battle about to take place, but I was extremely relaxed and focused.

After I put on my jock, T-shirt, and socks (always left sock first), I reached for my thermal sweatshirt but hesitated a second. It might show a sign of weakness to the cold, but I put it on anyway. I wasn't stupid. I put my thigh pads and knee pads into my pants. I shaved the thick pads with scissors until they were thin shells because that was the way Jim Brown did it. He wanted to be lean and fast. Me, too. Also, he did not wear rib or hip pads. All the offensive linemen did the same. We started wearing low-cut shoes just like Jimmy, too.

Running was our number one weapon. It set up our passing game. And what a corps of receivers we had! Collins, Warfield, Brown, Green, and Brewer. They all worked hard at it. I know Collins and Warfield would each catch fifty passes a day in practice. If they dropped even one, they would catch another ten!

My mind was reflecting on a lot of these things in the dressing room. It's funny, no one had any idea how much money this championship game paid. I was wondering what would have happened if I had pursued baseball. Would I have ever played in a World Series? I loved catching. Then I thought of the team party I arranged after the game. My wife and I might be the only two people there if things didn't turn out good. I had forgotten to ask how much the party room would cost or, for that matter, the cost of the band. Oh well, hopefully my game check would cover it. I had to forget about it. We had a game to play. We would know a lot of answers in about three hours.

After putting on my shoulder pads, Morrie Kono helped me with my jersey. John Wooten was dressing next to my locker when his shoestring broke. He said, "Morrie, I need a shoestring." Morrie always replied, "Left or right?" I chuckled to myself as I thought of Morrie's predictable sense of humor

It was about an hour before kickoff. Uncle Bill was still on the field moving around with his trusty camera. Monte Clark and I were chit-chatting about the condition of the field. If the temperature dropped much more, our cleats might not penetrate the turf, especially the frozen dirt in the infield area. We had our tennis shoes ready just in case, having remembered the year before, when the Chicago Bears changed their shoes during their NFL title game. They ended up beating the Giants.

Gene Hickerson was now on the field doing his regular pregame warm up, which consisted of nothing. He always stood leaning against the goal post watching everyone.

My mind drifted back to the prior year when I had been lucky enough to be selected for the first of my six straight Pro Bowl games. This year I had been voted to go again. And I was given the ultimate award by my teammates—most valuable player! The news media went nuts on this one. They chastised the players for picking me. How could they do such a stupid thing when Collins, Ryan, Groza, Warfield, Brown, and a lot of others, including several defenders, had had great seasons? How could they pick a lineman? I thought they were wrong to pick me, too. I don't know if all the media uproar had anything to do with it, but that was the last time the team ever gave that award.

The stands were now filling up, and the buzzing was getting louder. Most of the players from both sides were now on the field. Hickerson was still leaning against the goal post. I saw my wife and Mom in their seats. Dad seldom came—too much work back on the farm. I waved at them and they waved back. I felt good now that they were there. Mom was always early for the games. She carried an umbrella rain, snow, or sunshine.

Her seats were in the upper deck, right on the 45-yard line. She had an aisle seat with people always walking beside and in front of her. Occasionally someone would stop for a second or two, and she would poke them with her umbrella and say, "Move along! Move along!" She got into a few confrontations, but the ushers and police were aware of her actions and always came to the rescue.

Our entire offense seemed confident and ready. I still felt Blanton Collier had prepared us well. We finished our pre-game warm up as we ran about six plays against our defense before leaving the field for the dressing room. Of course, Futz was still telling me, "We're going to win, Schaf! We're going to win!" Now everyone in the locker room was going to the bathroom like me—about a dozen times so far. I had Morrie grease my uniform shoulders with Vaseline so it was hard for Brasse to try to grab hold of me.

I was thinking I would not have to worry about losing my usual twenty pounds on the field today. I had already lost that much emptying my bladder, and the game had not even started. An official yelled into our dressing room, "Hey, Coach, five minutes to go before game time!" Blanton wished us all good luck.

Now our captain, Galen Fiss, was talking. The room was really quiet. Galen was not a fireball speaker by any means—he was like Fred MacMurray (of *My Three Sons*), and we all really respected him. Galen gave a few last-minute reminders: We had won the coin toss, and our offensive team was to be introduced. Don't make any stupid mental mistakes today. Everyone be ready and alert to go into the game at any time. Let's overcome every setback. Replacement and starters, hustle on and off the field. Then we all knelt for the Lord's Prayer. Moments later, as we started walking through the long, narrow tunnel leading towards the field, I heard a lot of pads cracking (players hitting the cement walls with their helmets and pads). We were getting ready mentally and physically for what was about to happen. Our cleats clicked as we all walked along. The roar of the crowd was getting louder as we got closer to the field dugout. Someone was now yelling out our names to be ready for the introduction. I was nearly flying as I heard my name called. I swear my feet never touched the ground as I raced onto the field.

Coming out of that old dark tunnel reminded me of what it must have been like in Rome, when the gladiators appeared in the arena with thousands of screaming people ready for action.

What a thrill to be playing in front of more than 80,000 home fans in a championship game! I could still remember just ten years earlier going to the country store with my mom to watch the Browns championship game on a small black-and-white television. Next year (1965) would be the twentieth year of the Browns, and it would be their twelfth World Championship battle!

I prayed a short prayer to God, thanking Him for this opportunity to be part of this family and asking Him to please protect us all from injury and help us to play up to our potential. As they played the national anthem, I felt tears coming down my cheeks as I hummed the words. God, I loved this game!

Since we won the coin toss, we took the ball first, but Baltimore had an advantage: They chose to start the game with a strong northern wind at their backs. As the game went along, I kept thinking, thank goodness the Colts' offense was having a tough time. Our defense was fired up. Our offense couldn't get anything going either, but the Colts' offense was worse.

Bernie Parrish, our outstanding All Pro defense cornerback, had designed a bold, two-point plan to stop Unitas's passing game. It was totally unlike the way the Browns had played before. Howard Brinker had given him the okay to go ahead.

Bernie's first theory was that since the field was cold and partially frozen, it would take the effectiveness away from Baltimore's receivers, Jimmy Orr and Lenny Lyles, to make proper pass cuts. He and fellow cornerback Walter Beach challenged their receiver at line of scrimmage. They played every play like bears after honey. It confused Johnny Unitas.

The second plan was for our linebackers, Jim Houston and Galen Fiss, to play John Mackey, Baltimore's great tight end, head up when he lined up on one of their sides. Always play him tough like it's a run. Don't let him release to inside for a pass, thus taking away his favorite move. This also kept both linebackers in good position to defend against their Hall of Fame running back Larry Moore. Unitas was completely frustrated.

The Colts kept shooting themselves in the foot with fumbles, dropped passes, missed field goals and penalties. One reason was that Jim Kanicki was having a career game against their All-Pro guard Jim Parker. Kanicki was going after Parker like he was possessed. The whole defensive line kept playing a great game. Meanwhile, rather than being aggressive and going after them, our offense was playing not to lose. Their offense was definitely being outplayed on all fronts. The score at halftime was 0-0. In the dressing room I could hear our defense leaders yelling support for one another. They had the whole team excited. We had a lot of respect for them. They were a tough, smart, proud group.

Fortunately, our offense decided to stay with our game plan for the second half. With a new attitude and a few adjustments, we gained some consistency and started moving the chains. When you're in a struggle and nobody's giving anything, just keep the pressure on. It's like arm-wrestling—you keep pushing for your opponent to give first. Eventually somebody will gain an advantage. In the first half, we were playing well in two of the three phases of the game. Our offense, our biggest strength all season, was struggling. At the start of second half we were confident that we would be more consistent at moving the ball. Our defense had reassured us at halftime they would continue to stick it to them and added they would beat the Colts themselves if our offense couldn't score. What a challenge that was!

The crowd really got into it in the second half. The fans were roaring for blood! Thirty minutes to go. I was excited as heck! Brasse and I went at it again like two bulldogs during the second half. He was a tough, good player, but I refused to let him have an inch.

Our defense continued to shut them down. At halftime coach Nick Skorich told Parrish and Beach to keep doing what they were doing. Unitas will think you'll change the second half. Through the whole second half Baltimore kept waiting for them to back off. As the game went along our defense got more daring, using several all-out blitzes.

Our offense started the third quarter with the wind at our backs.

Galen Fiss made the play of the game. He tackled Lenny Moore on a screen pass with nothing between him and a sure touchdown. Years later, when Moore met Galen, he remembered the play. He said, "Mr. Fiss, I still can't believe it. How did you make that tackle?" Then Lou "The Toe" Groza nailed a field goal on his first attempt. We had broken the ice! I saw the glint in Collins's eyes as Ryan called his number on our next series of plays. Touchdown by Futz! 10-0! Jim Brown was running great, too. He almost broke it all the way twice. Ryan called for Collins's play again. He found him open. Touchdown! Wow! We were all going crazy now! Groza kicked another field goal. Next series, Collins again—his third touchdown! Ryan was throwing strikes. He was having a great game. We were up 27 to zip.

Defense. The defense had shut-out the mighty Johnny Unitas. I was so wrapped up in the offense that I was oblivious to the tremendous preparation of the defense.

Galen Fiss played his position with absolute perfection. When Galen hit Lenny Moore with that devastating tackle for a five-yard loss on a screen play, the impact drew oohs from the crowd. He also tipped a Unitas pass into the hands of linebacker Vince Costello for a great interception. It was Galen's day. The guys on defense thought he should have shared the MVP honors.

Big, young Jim Kanicki had the toughest assignment of the day. He was across from huge Jim Parker, later a Hall of Famer. Like Fiss, Kanicki had a career day. Weighing close to 290 pounds, Kanicki had youth on his side, and he nullified the Colts' offensive lineman for the game—a big factor in shutting down the Colts' running game.

Leroy Kelly was relegated to the special teams at this juncture. He had a sensational day with five or six crushing tackles, which stopped the Colts in their tracks on returns. Leroy also returned punts and kickoffs, each time bursting up field to put us in great field position, especially providing us with exceptional scoring positions in the big second half.

With Kanicki at defensive tackle teaming with veteran Dick Modzewelski, Paul Wiggin and Bill Glass were playing strong at defensive end, and Fiss, Costello, and Jim Houston were rock-solid at linebackers. In possibly their finest hour, the defensive backfield of Bernie Parrish, Ross Fichtner, Larry Benz, and Walter Beach shut down the Colts' receivers.

It was Johnny Unitas's worst nightmare as a quarterback—less than 100 yards passing. Howard Brinker had done a masterful job. Bernie Parrish's plan worked.

The officials let the clock run out for the last few minutes of the game. The fans were flooding the field for souvenirs, tearing down the goal posts, taking chairs, buckets, tape, even benches! I lost my chin strap.

Art's young nephew Dick Rosen, who assisted Morrie and Leo as their equipment watchdog, recalled asking Leo, "What should I do?" Leo yelled, "Forget everything—just leave it! Get to the dugout as fast as you can!"

We were partying in the dressing room. Fans were partying in the stands and in the streets. What a great feeling; we were World Champions! Thank you, Lord! I learned what "team" was all about. Gary Collins was right. He was named "Player of the Game" and presented the keys to a new Corvette.

There were lots of heroes: —the entire defense, especially Costello, Parrish, Beach, Fiss, and young Jim Kanicki. Lou Groza, at age forty, had two field goals and three extra points. Jim Brown gained over one hundred yards. Ryan was truly magnificent—three touchdown passes. Our offensive line played great. Ernie Green was doing his usual, throwing great blocks on runs and helping the line on pass protection. Everyone had played their hearts out. As the team knelt down to say a prayer of thanks, we could still feel the stadium shaking. Man, what a wonderful feeling!

For a short period of time, it was Camelot. There was bedlam in the dressing room after the game. Dick Modzelewski, covered with dirt and mud from head to toe, wrapped himself around sportswriter Chuck Such, who was wearing a new camel-haired overcoat. He didn't seem to mind.

Kanicki, wearing a huge smile, extended his arm, which was covered with blood from wrist to shoulder. "Isn't mine," the big tackle said, shaking my hand.

It was New Year's Eve, Christmas, the Fourth of July, and more all wrapped up into one explosive moment. There were bear hugs and more bear hugs. No one seemed to consider a shower.

"When we walked off that field, that moment took our emotions to heights we would never feel again the rest of our lives," said Paul Wiggin, describing the aftermath of the championship. "For ten minutes we peaked at such a crescendo emotionally that we felt like we owned the world." So we did. Forty years later I still try to relive that great feeling.

As I left the dressing room, I took one last look. Post-game newspapers were lying all over the floor with big headlines, "Browns Win World Championship." Blanton Collier was still chatting with some reporters, grinning from ear to ear. He stood up and gave me a big hug. I said, "I love you, Coach," and he replied, "Mule, I love you, too." We did his famous left-handed shake. (He always did that, he said, because the left hand is closer to the heart.) We both said, "See you at the Pro Bowl in a few days!"

Who would know that we would be the last Cleveland championship team. More than forty years ago. And there will never be a Super Bowl championship game played in Cleveland even if the Browns were to play in one. Today they're all played in warm weather states or domed stadiums.

I arrived at the party. It was football heaven! The whole team was there with their families and friends. Art Modell and all the coaches, including Blanton Collier and his wife Forman, showed up, too. For the record, Modell helped me to pay for the party. That night I thought I would play football forever! Why would I ever want to retire?

A BIG DISAPPOINTMENT

As big a thrill as 1964 was, the 1965 final at Green Bay was just as big a downer. We advanced to the NFL championship game with great expectations, but this time we lost to the Green Bay Packers, who were starting their four-year dynasty under Coach Vince Lombardi.

I believe that in 1964 and 1965 I played on one of the best Browns teams in history. I knew it was the best in all my thirteen years. I didn't get to play against the Packers in the '65 championship game; I had a torn hamstring and a hernia tear. John Brown, a fine tackle from Syracuse, replaced me and played well at my position. I thought we matched up well man-to-man. Give our offense the edge—give their defense the edge. For some odd reason, we allowed them to gain the mental edge on that day. I've always believed that 75 percent of the game is mental preparation. Instead of focusing in on everything, being totally positive, and playing aggressively and with intensity, we let little negative things creep into our heads. Like complaining that we were not playing before our home fans, that the turf was frozen, we were not wearing right the gloves, we were wearing the wrong shoes, our sideline heaters didn't work well. As you can see, these are all excuses. They should have been turned around and made positives.

For me, it was a sad day; I had to watch this championship game from the sidelines. It really hurt to miss this game—only the third one I had missed in my twenty years of playing high school, college, and pro ball.

The Pro Bowl in 1965 was Jim Brown's final farewell to football. Also, Frank Ryan was slightly injured in this same game by Baltimore Colts great defensive end Gino Marchetti, who was still upset over the 27-0 loss to us in Cleveland. Gino felt Ryan was trying to run up the score by still passing for a touchdown when the game ran out, and he was determined to make a statement by sacking him as hard as he could.

Afterwards, I spent a lot of time reconsidering my future. I was ready to retire. I was restless for a new challenge. Everything was happening so fast. The William Morris Agency in California took pictures of me and discussed a possible future in acting. They had me scheduled for auditions in military and western roles. I never tried it.

My Air National Guard supervisors and I discussed going to officer training school and getting back into the regular Air Force. Teammate Vince Costello and I started a boys' camp called Sky View, and at the same time Gary Collins and I started a corporation called Financial Planning. Also, I was questioning my marriage.

Since I was team captain I spent a lot of hours at Coach Collier's home discussing my feelings, my future, and being a team leader. A short time later Jim Brown retired, which really hurt. I stayed with the team six more years. I continued to struggle with myself and searched to fill some voids in my life. I was destined to make some bad decisions.

BERNIE PARRISH

Bernie Parrish was an All Pro cornerback from University of Florida. As a teammate, you always knew where you stood with him. He'd tell you. He was a talented, confident leader. I liked his style and respected him. One time he and his family drove to my parents' farm in Wooster to see all the animals and ride on the tractor. He got along with his teammates, and we voted him to be player representative for us in all union matters. He would meet with the teamsters on our behalf and campaigned regularly to have our team join them. He was labeled a born rebel because he wasn't afraid to say what he thought was right. I believe he enjoyed taking issues to the edge.

He made headlines in Cleveland when he called for the ouster of NFL Commissioner Pete Rozelle. This resulted in shortening his career considerably. A better term would be to say he was blackballed from playing with every team in the league.

As a player he was a captain on the field. He always relayed defense calls from the sideline coach to his teammates in the huddle. If he disagreed with their call he called his own. He made good decisions, and coaches went along with his behavior. But one time in the locker room, after we beat the St. Louis Cardinals, I witnessed Modell yelling at him because he made his own calls and not always those of the coaches. Vince Costello got in the middle of the argument and kept them apart.

Then it got ugly as Bernie wrote a book, *They Call It A Game*. He accused Modell of alleged association with mob figures and mentioned some of the crime people by name. Divorce was their only option.

Talking about Bernie, I recall when the NFL Players Association Pension Plan was started in 1959, my first year in the league. Bernie became our player representative early on. He was the lone ranger, constantly trying to get a handle on the future of the plan and the need for us to have strong representation from somebody like the Teamsters union. Now, forty some years later, there are hundreds of former (retired) veterans asking for better communication and representation.

Recently, I did some checking. According to the NFL Players Association audited accountant's report, as of March 31, 2006, there is over $900 million in net assets available for benefits already in the plan, and it's growing rapidly every year due to contributions from owners, TV, and various marketing contracts. The question is, what is the plan hoarding the dollars for? The pension was not set up for amassing a fortune for a few. The old-timers that helped start this great sport in the 1940s, '50s and '60s, and who are still living could use a little extra financial help.

It is embarrassing to compare our veteran benefits with those of the baseball players:

   a. Baseball—ten-year veteran, age 62—$175,000 per year income;
   b. Football—ten-year veteran, age 62—$39,920 per year income.

COACH COLLIER RIDES INTO THE SUNSET

Blanton Collier was a good teaching coach. It killed him when, in 1966, he was told not to teach anymore. Modell told him that a head coach had too many other responsibilities. It was a game of specialists. Most head coaches today don't teach much, either. They're mostly organizers, administrators, and motivators. Assistants do all the teaching.

What I've always felt bad about was the way Collier was let go. It hurt him to take over for Paul Brown, his long-time friend. He won a world championship and he played in another. He was in the hunt every year thereafter. Never had a losing season. After 1970, he was asked to step down because of an acute hearing problem, the result of a World War II injury. He just faded into the sunset. No retirement party. No front office job handling football operations or scouting. Just left Cleveland to never be seen in these parts again.

Nobody had an opportunity to say good-bye. A lot of coaches and players would often go to see him at his Texas home for advice. A year or so before his death I stopped in Houston to visit with him. There he was with that great big friendly smile. It was a great eight-hour visit, one I'll always cherish. He had a gigantic heart. The most loyal man God created.

A parting thought: Coach Collier should be in the Hall of Fame.

BLANTON'S WORDS OF ADVICE

It's amazing how much can be accomplished if no one cares who gets the credit.

Your performance should inspire your teammates.

A quarterback should call his own plays.

My players sometimes show the dog-gone-ist spirit and attitude I've ever seen.

The best way to stop blitzing is to run screens and draws.

It's hard to beat a team that won't give up.

The main ingredient of stardom is the rest of the team.

A perfect day is doing something for a person that will never be able to repay you.

CHAPTER SEVEN

WINDING DOWN

THE INFAMOUS GEORGE LAMB BET

In sports, as in life, you have your highs and lows. After we won the NFL title in 1964, I thought I'd play forever. But by 1971, the end of the road was in sight. I was hurting—physically and emotionally. The head slap had started to take its toll.

It was my thirteenth year with the Browns and Art Modell and I didn't agree on contract terms. The year before, I was asking for a three-year contract to play and help coach for $35,000, $37,500, and $40,000 respectively. Art offered one year for $33,000. I asked, "Is this your last offer?" He said, "Yes." I said, "Okay, I'll finish my career playing my option out." That was a mule-headed decision. I later found out that, under the NFL contract rules, if you play out your option, you have to take a 10 percent pay cut. As a matter of principle, I stuck with my decision. Most rookies were making more than that.

So, I started training camp with a $3,300 pay cut and a new coaching staff.

But what really hurt was a stunt I pulled about a month before camp: I ran sixty-two miles from Cleveland to Wooster. It started out as a bet I made with a local car dealer, George Lamb; in hindsight it helped to bring a quick end to my football career.

I bet George I could run nonstop from Municipal Stadium in Cleveland to Maurer Field, my old high school football field in Wooster. He said I couldn't do it and put a free car on the line. That was all I needed—a good challenge! Dan Coughlin, a writer for the *Cleveland Plain Dealer*, my radio disc jockey friend Jim Runyon, and popular Cleveland restaurant owner Pat McIntyre egged me on to do it. My youngest brother, Mike, volunteered to run with me for support.

As a special note: Mike was an extremely tough kid. He proved that early in life. We had a gravel driveway that came off the main road close to our house. One day, at age one and a half, Mike was outside playing in the gravel when Mom suddenly noticed he was turning blue and struggling to breathe. He had put a small stone in his mouth to suck on, and it was caught in his throat passage.

Mom tried everything to get it out. Nothing worked. She told Dad to call the hospital to let them know she would be coming as fast as she could. She put Mike in Sis's lap and away they sped off in our truck towards town. The doctors met her at the hospital door and immediately performed an emergency tracheotomy to take the stone out and inserted an air line into his throat so he could breath.

Sis said Mom was doing about 100 mph while they were both saying the rosary. God answered her prayers, and Mike was always her miracle boy. It took a year or so until he could get rid of the tube and eat and breathe normally.

I don't know why, but Mike and I have always been pretty close even though we're more than sixteen years apart. He is somewhat daring like me. If I said let's do it, he'd be ready to go now.

In any event, Mike and I were looking forward to our evening jog. We had planned our route weeks in advance. I weighed 255 and felt I was in pretty good condition. Unknown to us, this run was an obsession for George Lamb. His preparation was elaborate and precise. He had organized a steering committee months earlier that met weekly at Pat Joyce's tavern. He had formed subcommittees with different responsibilities—sheriff and police escort, departure plans, arrival party, publicity, media, medical, and refreshments.

Mike and I arrived at the old Municipal Stadium around 8 p.m. There was a crowd of about one hundred onlookers gathered to cheer us off. Soon after, the George Lamb Committee arrived dressed in full running gear, each carrying a cold can of beer. I quickly stepped into a nearby phone booth to shed my clothes. Alas, Superman appeared in pants and shirt. A stickler for details, Lamb talking over his speaker horn and made a historical announcement about the great run that was about to take place. Then, at the appropriate moment, he points to a bugler direct from Thistledown race track to blow the start—horse-race style. Yells and screams followed as we all trotted off up West 3rd Street. Two blocks later, Lamb's committee pulled off into a tavern for a drink. Mike and I were following a van driven by my wife loaded with emergency stuff, water, food, extra shoes, clothes, flashlights, bandages, etc. I told her we were going to cheat every once in awhile. I planned to jump into the back seat every five miles and rest for a mile or so. But before our first five-mile marker, the van started to overheat. Oh yes, I forget to mention that the van belonged to George Lamb. We did not see her again until forty miles down the road seven hours later! My cheating plan would not have worked anyway because Lamb had paid a deputy sheriff to follow me every inch of the road to Wooster.

Local high school track runners would appear and run with us a few miles in nearly every town we passed through. We never slowed our pace.

About forty-five miles and nine hours out, I started cramping and feeling a terrible pain in my neck, knees, ankles, and feet. Bad, constant pain. The pain went from the top of my head to the bottoms of my feet. Everyone, including George, was now begging me to stop. He said he'd still give me the car. It was already a great effort. But no, I was the Mule. I kept limping along.

Dad surprised us at the edge of Wooster. Mom had dropped him off to walk the final mile with us. What a picker-upper and encouragement that was. Dad's my hero.

At 11 a.m., fourteen and a half hours from when we started, Mike and I arrived at Wooster Maurer Field to a crowd of local cheerers. We waved and said thanks, but because of cramps and dehydration, I was put onto a stretcher by an emergency crew, slid into an ambulance, and driven directly to the hospital. I had lost nearly thirty pounds! They fed me fluids intravenously for a couple of hours. As I rested, I had a big smile from ear to ear—I kept thinking, car, I hope you're ready to travel!

MY LAST YEAR OF FOOTBALL

It was 1971. I was starting to mend when football camp opened four weeks later. But my legs were still rubbery, and the pounding on the pavement had caused pinched nerves to develop in my neck and shoulders. My right elbow still smarted from a torn tendon from 1969.

By this time, Nick Skorich was the new head coach, and Ray Prohaska was the new line coach. They had no sympathy for me especially since I was playing out my option. Coach Skorich didn't communicate very well with any of the older players and didn't mind telling us he was in the middle of a rebuilding process. It seemed from the get-go he wanted to clean house and start a youth movement. It was the first time I wasn't excited about being a Brown, but I accepted the new challenge and was ready to give my all for a great final season.

First day—Nick made everybody run a mile in six and a half minutes. If you couldn't do it, you had to run it every day until you got under that time. I made it with plenty to spare, but my legs were tight. It's funny thinking about it now, but Hickerson jogged the first hundred yards and then walked the rest of the mile. I think he finally jogged it all the way about a month later. Then Coach moved us right into 20- and 40-yard sprints for time. I asked him if I could sprint the following day because my legs were sore. He asked, "What do you think you are, a prima donna?" So I ran.

I had the fastest time for all the linemen for twenty yards. In the forty, I was okay for the first twenty yards, but then my legs locked up and I limped across the finish line with a time of 6.6 seconds. Normally, it would have been around 4.8. Coach says, "Boy, Schafrath, you've slowed down a lot!"

I know I didn't deal with this situation very well. I had always worked hard and proven myself on the field. I loved a coach who pushed me, but I was getting mixed signals. Besides, I refused to acknowledge that I was going to have to face retirement. I didn't know how to quit. I wanted to have a great season and help the team get to its first Super Bowl, but my every move was being degraded by my new coaches.

Next, we were tested with weights. Of course, I loved lifting weights, but with my injured elbow, I couldn't lift my own weight. Coach knew I had a bad elbow, but he remarked, "Don't seem very strong, Schafrath. Everyone has to be able to lift at least their own weight." There was a daily battle for a starting job at every position. I welcomed the challenge. After twelve years with the same plays I was comfortable, but now we had a new numbering system. Even-number plays were reversed to left side and odd-number plays went right. That kept me on my toes. Nevertheless, I was the starter when the season opened.

Then we were faced with a new environment. We moved to a new training facility once the season started. We went from soft grass at Don Fleming Field at Case Western Reserve University to hard Astroturf at Baldwin-Wallace University. My whole body ached from the moment I walked onto that new practice field.

For the first time, I started feeling daily burns in my neck and shoulders, then in my lower back and hips. When the burns hit me, it was like putting my finger in a light socket. For a second, I'd lose control of my whole body and fall to my knees. I was still practicing as hard as I could, but practice was not fun. It was constant pain. And of course, the defensive ends still used the head slap. Sometimes I had to sit in my car after practice for a while to try and relax before I could drive home.

In mid-season, we were in first place. One Monday as I came to practice, my teammates met me at the door with a copy of *The Plain Dealer*, which reported that four starters—Dick Schafrath, Bill Nelsen, Gary Collins, and Jim Houston—were being benched. Coach Skorich never said a word to me. He acted as if I was not on the team. I continued to practice and played on all the special teams. Doug Dieken, my replacement, did well. I gave him advice and pointers as often as I could. He soon developed into a great tackle. We made the playoffs that year but were stopped by the Miami Dolphins in the first game. That was the end of my career with the Browns.

I've heard it said many times—90 percent of professional athletes come in like heroes and go out as rats. I was put out to pasture for good.

THREE YEARS WITH GEORGE ALLEN AND
THE WASHINGTON REDSKINS

I was a free agent in 1972. I was depressed and feeling sorry for myself after what happened to me the year before. All of a sudden, George Allen, Washington Redskins coach, called to see if I was interested in being a player/coach. He offered me $100,000 for one year, a far cry from the measly $33,000 I earned my last year with the Browns. I said thanks, Coach, but no thanks because of the pinched nerve pain. But I asked him if I could get back to him if I ever changed my mind. It was hard to turn that deal down. I was a Browns player my whole life, but having a chance to play for a Super Bowl contender—wow!

Two years went by after retiring from football and I could feel the healing starting to take place in my neck, back, and legs. I started to feel good again. One day I called Coach Allen and asked if he was willing to give me another shot. He said, "Pass the physical, Dick, and you've got the same deal." I was as excited as a rookie!

In 1975 I arrived at their training camp at Carlisle, Pennsylvania, in pretty good shape. I passed the physical and practiced for the first week. Again, it was that hard Astroturf. I worked extra on my own each evening driving the blocking sled. I was penciled in to play some in the first Saturday scrimmage. As I was warming up on the hard surface, I got a hot burn in my neck and fell to my knees. It lasted a couple of seconds. It scared the heck out of me, but I didn't say anything to anyone. I told Coach Allen to forget playing me in that scrimmage—I wasn't quite ready.

After practice while in the dressing room, I got another hot burn. Again, I fell to my knees. The following morning I talked to Coach Allen. "Forget the playing, Coach, it's too risky." We tore up the contract, and I coached part-time with him for three years at $20,000 a year. I could have made $50,000 if I wanted to be a full-time coach.

George Allen was a winner. He was obsessed with winning! A great defense coach and a workaholic, he had an interesting sense of humor. He never tipped waiters or waitresses over fifty cents, no matter what the cost of the meal. Before one game, he put on war paint and a feathered Indian headdress, stood on a table in the middle of the room in front of the team, and did an Indian war dance, hollering and chanting and jumping around in circles.

In the airplane on road trips, he'd go up and down the aisle after wins leading us in different sing-a-long songs, particularly "Give Me That Old Time Religion." At the whole team meeting on Mondays, we would give stuffed animals as incentives to players leading the team in certain categories, like best hit, best run, best block, best catch, and so on. We did this for a year or so with the Browns. Guys would kill to get their names called! And they were all making six figures.

We'd be practicing sometimes, and he'd have the local fire department come in with sirens blaring and spray the team with water to cool us off. At times the police department would come buzzing in to provide us all with ice cream and pop. He'd do all kinds of crazy things. He was a defensive-minded coach. He was happiest if we could win 1-0. On offense, we seldom made any mistakes. We had a damn good team and I loved coaching with him. He asked me to go to the Rams with him in 1978.

People would ask why he kept bringing in old-timers rather than building his team with young draft choices. He always said, "The future is now. We don't have time to build a team with draft choices. You have to win now! Next game or next year is too late. Too many things can happen by long-term playing in contact sports."

I drove Coach Allen crazy. He prided himself in being the first person to arrive at practice in the morning and the last person to leave at night. He didn't know I was staying in the weight room. It was my home for the season. He always arrived at 7 a.m. I could hear him coming through the gate, and I'd get up, jump on an exercise bike, and start working out. After a couple of weeks, he was coming earlier and earlier to beat me. One morning he was in at 5 a.m. and still too late! I found him asleep in his chair at midnight with the film projector still running. I finally discovered that what he was doing was because of me. I told him, "Coach, I don't know whether you know this, but I'm staying here at the facility." He let out a big sigh of relief. He went back to his normal schedule, 7 a.m. arrivals and 9 p.m. departures.

I still regret not going with him to the Rams.

LIFE OUTSIDE
THE LINES

CHAPTER EIGHT

VIETNAM

I played in a Rose Bowl and felt an unforgettable rush of adrenalin from the wild-cheering, frenzied crowds packing the Ohio State stadium as the band's heart-pounding music blared.

I thrilled to the thunderous cheers rained down from more than 80,000 rabid fans each week when I played for the Cleveland Browns. Those echoes live on.

I still feel goose bumps when I recall the excitement after winning the 1964 World Championship.

I've received standing ovations after motivational speeches.

But, nothing—*nothing*—compares with the most indelible experience of visiting our military people in Vietnam during that war.

Those are the real heroes.

I wish I could have brought every one of them into Cleveland or Columbus to receive and hear the cheers of 100,000 people. They deserved it. I'll never forget them.

In 1969, I volunteered to go to Vietnam on a USO tour. They say you shouldn't volunteer for anything concerning the army. A few dozen medical shots and a ton of paperwork later, I was on the twenty-hour trip by Air Force military troop carrier. We flew into the teeth of a wicked storm over the Pacific. It was the first time I prayed anything other than the rosary. Several times I was sure the plane was going down. With eyes closed, I prayed, "Lord, please be with me if it's my time." Beside me was a large box of approximately 10,000 Browns NFL stickers that my wife suggested I purchase. They were blessed many times and well received. Other NFL players on the trip were Tommy Nobis (Falcons), Joe Namath (Jets), Al Atkinson (Jets), Dan Reeves (Cowboys), Billy Ray Smith (Colts), Irv Gross (Eagles), and Bill Grantham (NFL office).

Arriving at Saigon, we were taken to a hotel, our new home base for the next few weeks. Everyone was issued army gear to wear if we so liked, Then it was off to our mission to visit army hospitals and troop bases most every day.

During the day we usually traveled in threes visiting tent hospitals with our army guide in a jeep or helicopter. In the evening, we tried to calm down and reflect on and share our experiences. Sometimes it was too difficult to talk about. One medical officer said they performed two hundred amputations the previous month.

Coach Woody Hayes sure made a big impression and was liked here. The fellows said he stuck to the same game plan as he did in football. Coach stayed on the ground 93 percent of the time. He didn't like to fly.

Our involvement in this war was like coming into the ball game in the fourth quarter, ten touchdowns behind with no game plan to win. Rules changed daily in regard to what our soldiers could and could not do. It was America's first war experience with terrorists. You did not know who your enemy was—everyone looked the same. Men, women, and children that worked around you during the day might be trying to kill you at night. The Vietnamese are small people, averaging five feet tall, 120 pounds. Prostitution was legal. Many children pimped for their moms; they would stand in front of a shack and say, "Want a virgin? Only $5."

Everyone had a bicycle. Well, maybe not everyone. I once counted ten people riding on one bike! There were a hundred motorbikes to one car in every village and city. The streets were always jammed. Traffic lights seldom worked. My favorite thing to do in Saigon was to ride in a rickshaw, a two-wheeled cart pulled by a taxi runner.

Most homes were small huts made out of grass, sticks, and mud with dirt floors. Pigs and chickens lived in the same house with people. Few had electricity, no one had running water. They drank, bathed, and went to the bathroom in water streams that animals also used. The temperature averaged over 100 degrees year round. Rat meat was a delicacy. Open-air, non-refrigerated, crowded food markets were down every street. Animals and birds were sold live. Education and schooling was minimal, mostly for the elite.

We were warned not to drink their water, not to trust anyone, and not to travel in groups larger than four. The Viet Cong would tie live grenades to children or women and send them into crowds to sacrifice themselves. Great celebrations and carnivals were rewards for death. It was sacred, religious, and holy to sacrifice your life for your country. Sound familiar?

In most wars our country has been involved in, it's always been man-on-man, tank-against-tank, plane-against-plane. Fight to the end. Try to crush the enemy into submission. Not stopping until total victory. But this was not a typical war. It was a game of cat and mouse. Booby traps and land mines. The enemy seldom travels in large numbers. When they do, they try to overrun you faster than you can shoot them. Sometimes soldiers and their entire families would be together. Find them, chase them, shoot them. Children and women got hurt, too. They grew up in these hills, swamps, and jungles. They knew where to hide—in churches and off fighting limit providences and into nearby countries. They were experts at deceptive devices of all kinds. Charley (Viet Cong) could exist on nuts, fruits, leaves, and other natural things. It was hard for our soldiers to adapt and fight the same way. The circulated daily news we saw was the media criticizing our soldiers for being there and people back home demonstrating and protesting.

Our young soldiers remained loyal and committed. Daily many of our army and marine ground troops would travel in small groups of ten to twelve on search-and-destroy missions looking for signs of the enemy in the jungles, swamps, and caves. One person was the point man, always in front, while others were spread out like a diamond following close behind. The point man was responsible for the safety of his group. Once contact was made, he would call for outside reinforcements. These groups were great team players; they had to be—their very existence depended on each other.

When we'd meet soldiers, they'd listen to our every word. You'd bond immediately. You hated to leave them. They seemed so young, innocent, and brave. We're all family. They didn't like talking about themselves. Just things back home like sports, movies, girls, and especially Mom and Dad.

I met one boy who was to be transferred to a hospital in Japan as soon as they could get a chopper for him. Just hours before, he had lost a leg, both hands, and some other body parts from a grenade. He told me, "Mr. Schafrath, I'd sure hate to have to play football with all those big mean guys! How did you do it? Aren't you scared?"

Another guy was covered with a lot of tape, gauze, and cloth pads from his waist to the top of his head. He had received horrible burns from a napalm bomb. There was no skin left on his face or ears. His arms were tied to the bedsides so he would not touch or scratch himself. Full of morphine, he wanted a puff on a cigarette. I said, "I have none." He asked me to say a prayer for him. I said, do you have a rosary? He said, "No. Please just pray, sir." I said, "Lord Jesus, please be with Joe today. He needs you." That's all I could think of. I repeated those words over and over again until he went to sleep. Talk about guts. War is hell! Try to think how horrible that would be for anyone to endure, especially someone nineteen years old with his whole life ahead of him. We'd see hundreds of these wounded, brave young men every day. Another depressing thing occurred each day—mail call. It was tough to watch. Guys standing with their heads bowed, hoping to hear their name called. Maybe one hundred people standing, but only a handful got a letter. Then the slow walk back to whatever they were doing. When I arrived home, my wife and I immediately did a letter campaign for Vietnam soldiers through a local Cleveland radio station. Thousands of letters were sent to us by people that cared enough to want to help. We sent bushel baskets full to Vietnam from caring Americans who wanted to help our troops at mail call.

Our days were from 5 a.m. to 6 p.m. My pilot was an eighteen year old from Oklahoma named John Mays. His code name was "Sloopy." Lt. Mays helicoptered me all over Vietnam. He was super! We saw a lot of cities, including Saigon, Danang, Hue, Khesanh and Dakto. We saw the Mekong Delta, the DMZ, Ho Chi Minh Trail, and la Drang Valley. These places all became everyday names. We touched a lot of lives. I sometimes rode as Sloop's co-pilot, and he would let me have the controls. I also rode as the machine gunner on the outside. I fired it a lot, too! I understand why Woody Hayes, Bob Hope, and many other athletes and entertainers kept going back with the USO year after year to encourage our fighting forces. I had the opportunity to fly on and off three large aircraft carriers, the U.S. Hancock, the U.S. Kitty Hawk, and the U.S. Ranger, in a winged aircraft. Boy, was that an experience. Cable stopped you one second on landing. On take off, you were airborne in three seconds. They were part of the Navy's 7th Fleet stationed in the China Sea. My fellow teammates and I spent a lot of time talking football with navy seamen. They were all great sports fans. The carriers were all like floating cities with their own radio and TV stations. Food—all you could eat twenty-two hours a day with two hours to reload. The confusing thing for me was to know where I was going with sixteen decks of floors. If you want to get in shape, try getting around all day without an elevator. I got lost one time after asking directions to the latrine. For the next half hour I was like a small child lost in a supermarket. There was an all-alert for me on the ship, announcing my name every twenty seconds. I knew who and where I was, but no else did. Eventually, security did find me. I was quite embarrassed. After a day or so, the rolling seas started getting to me. I was begging to get my feet back on solid ground.

I met actor Jimmy Stewart one night at our Saigon hotel. He jumped out of his chair so fast to say hi that it startled me. He did that for every person—stood up, looked you in the eye, and speaking gently and politely while shaking your hand. His wife traveled with him daily. She wore a fatigue jacket with every badge and metal imaginable pinned to it. She was covered back and front. Of course, I pinned a Browns sticker on her, too. The soldiers loved giving them their badges. They both wore them all proudly every day.

I asked Mr. Stewart how I could get a guardian angel to serve me like he had in the movie, "It's a Wonderful Life." He said, "It's easy. Just get on your knees and pray a prayer of thanks for what you already have." I also asked him if it was fun to do the Glenn Miller story. He said it was because he admired Mr. Miller's talent so much, and he got a chance to learn a few notes on the piano, too.

He gave me his private phone number in California, but I never had a chance to call him.

I spent time with Hank Williams, Jr., too. He sure didn't look much like his father with the beard and all. He was a real polite gentleman. I shared how much I loved hearing his father sing country. And that he died much too young. He said he hardly knew him.

The majority of our soldiers were recent high-school graduates—very few from college or wealthy families. All lived by Semper Fi, one for all and all for one. Every soldier's life was changed forever by his experience in Vietnam. Many kept re-upping to go back with their buddies who were still there. There were no cheerleaders sending soldiers to Vietnam and no cheerleaders, other than family, welcoming them home. I'm proud to be an American and proud of every person who spent one minute in Vietnam. They were all heroes. And the same can be said for anyone who has ever served in the armed forces.

My cousin, Captain Tom Moritz, served two tours of duty in Vietnam as an Air Force pilot. He's still suffering from the affects of Agent Orange. My brother Ed was in Vietnam, too—until he was wounded by a grenade. He relayed an interesting story to me. As he and his search and destroy team came across an orphanage in the jungle, there were at least three hundred kids and just three nuns taking care of them. He said, "Sisters, do you have everything you need?" They said, "We're okay, soldier, but thanks for asking." They did share one need he could not give them: The children's number one cause of death was loneliness. They did not have time to give all the kids enough love and attention. Loneliness. That had to be a horrible way to die.

After nearly two months in Vietnam, I arrived in Hawaii for a week's R&R before flying back to Ohio. That evening, after my first good American meal, I went back to my room to relax. I discovered I had been burgled. My suitcase and large satchel loaded with souvenirs from our soldiers were stolen out of my room. I was so upset that I got on the next flight and flew home.

CHAPTER NINE

POLITICS

RONALD REAGAN

In July 1976 I got a call at my home in Loudonville at 9 a.m. on a Saturday morning. When I left the Browns, I bought a canoe livery in Loudonville, Ohio, about sixty miles south of Cleveland, and it was keeping me as busy as heck. Lots of people were coming, and it was going to be a beautiful, sunny, hot day. Just the perfect kind of day you want if you own a canoe livery! I get this call from somebody in Cleveland, Ohio. He said he was a front man working for the committee to elect Ronald Reagan for president of the United States. He wanted me to come to Lakewood Park that afternoon and say a few welcoming words to Mr. Reagan and some other dignitaries traveling with him. I told the man I was sorry, but I couldn't do it as it was a very busy day for me. About two hours later, I got another call from the same guy. He really wanted me to be there in the worst way. I told him to phone someone else; I was busy as heck and couldn't afford to leave and drive an hour and a half to Cleveland.

By this time, it's 1:30 in the afternoon and we are really busy! We have people waiting in lines to go canoeing, and I'm sweating like a stuffed hog, running all over the place, helping people. The phone rings again. It's this same guy, and he is desperate. "Please come," he just kept saying. He needed me to be there in the worst way. I finally called two of my brothers and asked if they could please help me out since I had to be in Lakewood at five o'clock. Thankfully, they both said yes.

There were an estimated ten thousand people picnicking at the Lakewood event. I made my wife Judy go with me, and we raced to

Cleveland. I had on a white T-shirt, some muddy blue jeans, and dirty tennis shoes. I did not have time to shower or shave. Since my hair was straggly, I had a baseball cap on backwards. We arrived at 4:45 p.m.

The park was packed with people as my wife and I tried to make our way through to the stage area. There was a Salvation Army pep band sitting behind the stage area. No one else was there. I kept trying to find someone in charge, but no one was there. There was a mike, a podium, and some speakers on the stage. The band asked me what they should do. I said, "Why don't you play some peppy, patriotic songs until someone in charge shows up?" They thought that was a good idea and started playing. Judy and I were sitting on the edge of the stage relaxing, chewing gum, arms folded, our legs swinging.

About ten minutes later, a long motorcade with eight police cars leading six limousines enters the park. I thought to myself, what the heck is happening? Where are the people in charge? This must be Mr. Reagan coming to the stage area, but there is no one here but the Salvation Army band and me to greet and introduce him. I said, "Judy, whoever is running this program must be in the vehicles with them."

I decided to act like I saw something behind me and stood up. I told the band to keep playing, and I threw as many chairs as I could onto the stage while Judy started setting them up. Then I jumped in front of the mike and said, "Ladies and gentlemen, the next president of the United States, Ronald Reagan!" Onto the stage comes a parade of people. I said, "Judy, please stand by me and help. I think some of them are movie stars." Thank God she watched old movies and TV; she knew all of them. Fess Parker, Jimmy Stewart, Tony Martin, Doris Day, Cyd Charisse, Charlton Heston, Kirk Douglas, and on and on. I then asked everyone to stand and say the Pledge of Allegiance with me. Judy stood in front of the stage facing me and lip-synced the words so I wouldn't make a mistake. They all sat down on the stage and looked me up and down like I was from another planet. I smiled, put my hat on backwards and, thanks to my wife, called each of them to the mike by their correct name to say a few words. I guess the event was a success. Mr. Reagan shook my hand and said I did a fine job. I never did know who called me or who was in charge of that event.

The next time I saw Mr. Reagan was in 1983 during his presidential re-election campaign. How could he forget me? He called me the "cowboy from Ohio." We had a good laugh about that Lakewood event. He still remembered my outfit and referring to him as the Gipper! He won re-election in a landslide, carrying forty-nine states. My two daughters, Renée and Heidi, attended the Inaugural Ball with me.

HOW I GOT INTO POLITICS

I got my first real taste of politics around 1983. I had helped President Nixon in the past, and I helped Ronald Reagan during his unsuccessful presidential bid in 1976 and again when he won in 1980. In 1983, Lynn Nofsinger called to see if I'd help in Reagan's re-election bid in the spring. Ed Rollins and Lynn were the campaign strategists, and I became their national chairman of athletes and entertainers. I traveled to the Washington office every week, helping put together athletic tours in all fifty states that election year. I. We solicited over five thousand athletes, people like Cathy Rigby, Mickey Mantle, Roger Maris, Joe Frazier, Stacey O'Neil, Woody Hayes, Joe Paterno, Roger Staubach, Bart Starr, Ron Kramer. We'd get on a bus and go into towns all across America. We'd blitz a town for an hour signing autographs, then go up and down the streets wearing "Vote for Reagan and Bush" T-shirts before jumping back in the bus and going on to the next town. We blew people's minds.

Jump to June 1985. I was in Wyoming with two of my sons, Ty and Bruin, looking into the possibility of managing a cattle ranch close to Saratoga, Wyoming. I had some contacts through a good friend of mine, Jess Bell, the "czar" of athletic feats. No one could run distance better. He owns a women's cosmetics company, Bonnie Bell, in Rocky River, Ohio. We were at this ten-thousand-acre ranch helping dehorn, castrate, and brand calves when an elderly gentleman rides up on a horse and asks if there was someone there by the name of "Schadack" from Ohio. I said, "Close enough. That's me."

He said there had been a phone call for me. Since there was no phone on the ranch, he asked me to jump on the back of his saddle and ride with him to the nearest phone. I was to make a call to long-time friend Billy Long in Columbus, Ohio. I wondered how he found me. He and another friend, Bob McEaneney, learned that a state senator from my home district had retired in the middle of his term to pursue another career. The Senate leadership was interviewing possible candidates to take his place. My two friends thought I would be a good choice. I said to them, "Who's Paul Gillmore, Stan Aronoff, Paul Pfeiffer, Dave Hopson, and Richard Finan?" I had never heard of these people before. They said that they were all Republican Senate leaders. I then called my good friend, State Representative Tom Van Meter, to ask him what he thought I should do. He said, "I would recommend that you come back and explore the possibility, and go through the interviewing process. It would be a good experience," even though he thought he might retake the job himself since he was a senator before.

That was the last time Tom and I ever talked. As it turned out, he did want the job himself. Tom was a highly decorated veteran from the Vietnam War. Awarded Purple Heart for bravery. He was a hard-working, conservative Republican legislator, good friends with conservative congressman John Ashbrook, who died while in Congress. Many state legislators were in office because of Tom's help. He was a great friend of Governor Rhodes, President Nixon, and Woody Hayes. He and his wife Nancy had two beautiful daughters. I helped him during his unsuccessful bid for governor in 1982. He helped me get the job in Washington as National Chairman of Athletes and Entertainers for the 1983 Reagan and Bush re-election campaign.

Still in Wyoming, my thirteen-year-old son Bruin and I went bear hunting (with no weapons) so I could relax and think. He was too young to know any better. Ty was nineteen and a little wiser. He thought we were both crazy and wouldn't go along. Luckily we didn't encounter any bears even though there were bear warning signs everywhere. The next day all three of us went rattlesnake hunting. That is a great sport, too—especially when you're scared to death of snakes and don't know what you're doing in those hills. Luckily we didn't encounter any snakes either. The following day I called another close friend, Pat Leahy, for his advice. He said, "You should get your butt back to Ohio and do it, Schaf. You don't have anything to lose." My sons and I worked on the ranch for a couple more days. Then I decided we should drive back to Columbus for the interview before deciding whether to take the ranching job.

We drove nonstop back to Columbus. Pat said to stop at his home before going for the interview. He needed a couple hours with me to go over some things that might help. The interview was scheduled for 9 a.m. I arrived at Pat's a little late—8 a.m. I only had about half an hour. Pat quickly gave me some important facts and figures about my district and each of the Republican leaders' districts—things about index numbers, etc. They were Greek to me. But I wrote important things down in the palm of my left hand and on my wrist. That helped me remember some football plays when I was with Ohio State and Browns. Why shouldn't it work in politics? Pat scratched his head and wished me luck.

Senators serving on the selection committee were Stan Aronoff, Dave Hopson, Bob Ney, Paul Gillmore, and Paul Pfeiffer.

The interview went well. Afterwards, I called Pat to thank him, and he said that I should not stop there. He said, now call on all the other Republican senators, ask to meet with them, and ask for their support. I said, "What number should I give them to call me back if they're not in?" He gave me a number, then said I should get to his office immediately. His office was actually with State Auditor Tom Ferguson—a Democrat, and the phone number was Mr. Ferguson's private number. No one other than Pat knows this story. Anyway, I was chosen to be a senator the next day.

Bill, Bob, Pat, and I still laugh about that day. I was never in politics one day before being appointed. It's kinda like playing in the Super Bowl the first time you try the game, then spending the rest of your life learning how to play.

Immediately after my appointment, the Senate leaders put me

on a crash course on how to be re-elected in 1986. They assigned me a full-time live-in tutor named Tom Pappas. He was raised in Doylestown, a city in my district. Tom was a young, good-looking, no-nonsense, executive type guy. Energetic, highly intelligent, and a college grad, he was pursuing a law degree with political aspirations. With my background and lifestyle, we couldn't be more opposite, but that was his problem. His career depended on getting me re-elected. He had to pray I'd be a quick learner.

No one at that time knew for sure whether Van Meter would challenge me in the primary, but it was suspected. The polls at that time showed that if he did run, he would beat me 70-30. We had a lot of work to do for the next fifteen months besides doing regular Senate duties. In addition to that, I continued to own the canoe livery, which required my presence from the middle of April to the middle of October.

From the start it was 24/7, traveling one hundred to five hundred miles per day. Tom and I attended every type of function we could find in my district, political or not. If a few people were in an open area or barn, we stopped by. Pappas slept on floors, couches, chairs, and sometimes in the car. He was something special. After a while he grew on me, and I liked his style—nervous but stabling. I actually saw a poker face smile on a couple of occasions. We both had a hard time finding time to wash our clothes. If they got too dirty or smelly, we'd just switch underwear. When Van Meter declared his candidacy, the official war began!

It was the most expensive and hard-fought primary the state had ever seen. Each side raised and spent over a million dollars. The job only paid $22,000. Something seemed wrong.

My three co-chairmen were my father, Woody Hayes, and Paul Brown. Steadily coming from behind on election night, we won by a few votes. (I think it was 120!) I had a lot of help from both Democrats and Republicans. Since that first primary, I have never spent more than $20,000 for any primary and general election put together. My favorite door-walking partner aside from my children and Tom Pappas was Debbie Bramlage. She and my daughter, Heidi, walked miles and miles. Debbie still works in the Senate offices. I always enjoyed walking door-to-door, meeting folks and doing debates. A pig could win an election if you spent enough money on TV, radio, and newspaper advertisements. People vote on perception and rhetoric. Van Meter's biggest weakness was his attitude. Always negative, he seldom smiled or laughed.

MORE THAN A DEBATE

Tom Pappas and I still agree that the highlight of my Senate campaign was a debate between Van Meter and me. The Loudonville Chamber of Commerce chose a small, vacant, former grocery store as a location for the evening debate. It was a cold night, and I remember the windows being frosted because there were so many people jammed into the room. Van Meter and I kept the timer person busy all evening as we both constantly ran over our allotted three-minute limit answering questions. Lots of good punches were scored by both.

Although there were countless things I could cite regarding the debate, how it concluded is the most memorable. We each had two minutes of closing remarks. Van Meter went first and, as usual, threw everything at me, including the kitchen sink. I was accused of not paying taxes, having both a failed business and two failed marriages, and lying to voters. He took the entire two minutes to unload his guns on my character, personality, family, and entire way of life.

When it was my turn to give concluding remarks and respond to the attacks, I looked around at the crowd (whose jaws remained dropped), paused, and said, "Since a lot has been said throughout this hard-fought campaign, and particularly during this evening's debate, especially the most recent by Van Meter, I feel the best way to end everything is with a prayer."

The audience, the media, and all the other local politicians were completely taken off guard by my desire not to defend myself. (Woody Hayes always said to me, if you don't have anything good to say about somebody, shut up.)

Equally memorable was what occurred later that evening when

members of my campaign cabinet met to review the happenings and discuss what we were going to do at our breakfast debate the next morning in Wooster. Pappas and I were sitting around my kitchen table with long-time Republican strategists Jim Tilling and Kurt Steiner. I was tired from the Loudonville shoot-out and feeling burned out from the entire day's activities, let alone the wear and tear of the long campaign. We were trying to focus on what I did well and poorly during the debate, and I was trying to get focused on issues and points for the next morning.

Rubbing my eyes and running my fingers through my hair, I said, "Men, I can't do this right now, My brain is a sponge."

Tilling, Steiner, and Pappas were taken aback by this comment. After a few moments of silence, Steiner looked seriously into my face and said, "As long as you are a candidate and a state senator, I don't want you to ever use the words 'brain' and 'sponge' in the same sentence again!"

SERVING THE DISTRICT

As a senator I traveled about 60,000 miles a year serving 350,000 people in my district. (We have term limits here in Ohio, and I was termed out in 2001.)

I always liked helping people, and I never got too high or too low about my job. I know playing sports taught me to keep a proper perspective about being in the public eye. You can be a hero or goat in a matter of seconds. Also, there is a limit to what you can do helping people. You can work twenty-four hours a day and still it's not enough.

An army major in Vietnam once told me, We do the difficult everyday; the impossible takes a little longer. I thought of that many times serving in the Senate.

Also, to me, some of the laws we make are like making sausage on butchering day. If you saw how it's made you wouldn't like it. Most verbal agreements were something you never could rely on.

In earlier days, legislators had full-time occupations at home. Drive to Columbus maybe three months a year to do political business. Kinda like when I first played with the Browns, football was part-time job for three months.

First disagreement I had was with a Democrat in committee. He said to me, let's take a break and start back with a better attitude. He then added, I'll hug your elephant if you kiss my ass!

I learned there are two kinds of legislators: show horses and workhorses. If you want your name in the paper, be a show horse. If you want the respect of your colleagues, be a workhorse.

A fellow senator gave me this advice my first day on the job. One difference between politics and football: to score points in football you have to move the ball from end zone to end zone. In politics you get more done working between the 40s. Getting bills to the end zones takes too long.

EXCITING DEBATES

One day during a Senate Republican Caucus session, Gene Watts and Tim Greenwood started fighting with each other. I dove into the middle to break it up. I ripped my pants from one end to the other and had to go around that way the rest of the day. Kinda breezy-like!

Another time during a debate, the opportunity arose for me to use one of my favorite arguments from Abe Lincoln's book of political stories. When someone has a weak argument that hardly makes sense, come back at them with this one. "Sir, that argument has about as much substance as a bowl of homeopathic soup made out of the shadow of a starved-to-death sparrow." Our debate ended with my opponent's mouth open in puzzlement. Then he said, "That was a good one, Schaf."

APPEARANCE COUNTS

I was a little late getting to many of my engagements because of the large district I had to cover (five and one-third counties). To save some time, I learned to change my clothes while driving my car. That's quite a feat!

One time I was helping my dad on his farm. I had an appearance that evening and, in a hurry, I picked up Dad's suit and shirt by mistake. I have an eighteen and one-half inch neck; he had sixteen. I wear a forty-six-long suit; he wore forty-four regular. Somehow I got it on before going inside the building. The pants were about a foot above my shoes and I had no socks on; I looked like a clown. The funny thing was, nobody said anything! I guess I looked normal.

One year during a Senate race, I arrived at my eleventh appearance about an hour late. One person was still there; he appeared to be a farmer. He was wearing cowboy boots, a ten-gallon hat, and was chewing on a piece of straw. I said, "I'm sorry I'm late, sir, but since you're still here, I'm going to give you the best speech I can for the next fifteen minutes." He nodded for me to start. When I finished, I said, "I'm sorry, sir, but this has been one of the longest days of my life, and I think I'll just move on out of here and go home." The gentleman jumped up and said, "Senator, I waited for you quite a while tonight. Now please, sit down. You see, I'm the last scheduled speaker, and now you'd better sit and listen to me." I stayed for another half hour.

MEDIA

After a particularly controversial bill was signed into law by my fellow senators and me, reporters were eagerly looking for someone to quote. Everyone had hurried out of the room, and I found myself cornered by a group of reporters who demanded that I give them a comment. "Senator Schafrath, what do you think? Any comments?" According to a *Cleveland Plain Dealer* writer, I said, "Okay, ladies and gentlemen, I'll be truthful but brief. I'd say we just screwed the people in this state equally from both sides of the aisle."

I AIM TO PLEASE EVERY CONSTITUENT

Before I had an answering machine, I once got a call from an eighty-plus-year-old young lady. It's two o'clock in the morning. She says, "Is this Senator Schafrath?" I said, "Yes, ma'am, this is he." She says, "Can you help me? Please?" I said, "What's your problem?" She says, "I've got water coming through my ceiling." I said, "Did you call a plumber?" She says, "Yes, but all I get is an answering machine." Then she said, "I called the sheriff, but the sheriff said to call your state senator!" I said, "Okay, ma'am, where do you live?" She told me where, some place five miles out in the country. So I told my wife, "Honey, I don't know how to fix anything; you know that. But with my luck, I've got to go give her moral support."

So, loaded with my hammer, screwdriver, and crescent wrench, I get to her house and, sure enough, water is coming down through the ceiling. She had a plunger for me, and I went upstairs and plunged. She was a Democrat and I'm a Republican, but she said, "Senator, I don't care what you are, but I'm going to vote for you from now on!"

I liked her style. I believe that's the way it should be. Vote for the person, not the party.

JOB SECURITY—ROCK ON!

After two years in the Senate, the president of Ohio State University's branch facility in Mansfield gave me a gift to use in my office. It was a nice wooden rocking chair with a sales tag still tied to the handle. It said guaranteed ten years. I thought that message would be a good omen. I never took the tag off. I made it sixteen years.

NOTHING GETS IN MY WAY WHEN IT COMES TO WORK

One morning I came into the state capitol building at 7 a.m. to find a real live doe trotting down the hall towards me. She went into my office. She did some damage as she was scared to death, but we got the Humane Society to come and help me take her safely out of the building. She was taken to the country.

One winter morning when I was staying at my friend Pat's house (about four miles from the State House), I didn't realize it was twenty-two degrees below zero! I couldn't start my car. I didn't know it wouldn't start because of the extreme cold. I started walking to the State House thinking I'd get a cab or bus soon. None were running—too cold. Everything in the city was shut down except emergency vehicles. I did not have a cap, gloves, or boots. I made it about an hour and a half later. Ice covered my face, hair, and hands. It took me another hour to thaw out! I was the only member to show up for that morning's committee meetings.

JIM BROWN: STILL TOUGH

One project I was proud to be involved with was Jim Brown's Amer-I-Can program.

Jim started the program around 1990 He believed that with self-determination, kids and adults could learn positive life skills. It covers things like responsibility, caring, confidence, respect, feelings, and having a positive attitude—things they never learned at home, especially without two parents teaching them.

I discovered that Jimmy's program had the respect of most of the gang leaders in the Los Angeles area, and he was asked by the mayor to act as a mediator in gang warfare. I've been at his house when the Bloods and the Crips would come for their pow-wows. They were always welcome, but they had to check any weapons at the front door. "Throw 'em in that basket," Jim would tell them.

Sometimes the meetings would take place mid-day, but in most instances it was after dark. The lights would be down real low and about all you could see were eyeballs. They'd start complaining about what another member of a gang did. "You stabbed my brother seven times" or "You raped my mother" . . . "Oh yeah, well you cut my sister up" or "You shot and killed my father."

Sometimes, they'd start shouting at each other or one of them would push another. Jim would step in and say, "Cool it!" He'd let them air it out and that helped reduce some of the tensions. They trusted him, and he trusted them.

Gangs today come in all colors and nationalities—Whites, Blacks, Asian, Jewish, Mexican, Latino. And Jimmy relates to all of them. Today, his Amer-I-Can program is in about twenty states, including some Ohio schools. At first, teachers were reluctant to have ex-gang members as facilitators in the schools, but now most welcome them because they can relate and help with the "troublemakers." His program is really powerful and should be taught to all middle school kids. I feel it teaches the foundation of traditional principles and values this country was built on.

I helped to get the program funded while I was in the senate. I think it helped contribute to better morale, better attendance, better grades, and a decrease in violent behavior. Sadly, Ohio's funding for Amer-I-Can was immediately dropped after I retired.

DINING AT THE WHITE HOUSE

Jan and Mary Jean Rus were wonderful friends who lived in the Washington, D.C., area. Jan worked for the United States government for thirty to forty years. He had formerly lived in California and worked for the Los Angeles Rams.

I helped President Nixon in his election bid early on here in Ohio. Nixon had developed a close friendship with Coach Woody Hayes back in the 1950s, and he remained a big Buckeye supporter until his death. Jan invited Judy and me to attend dinner at the White House with President Nixon and several of his guests. The year was 1972. I remember at our table was Cyd Charisse, Tony Martin, Jimmy Stewart, and a couple other movie stars. All the men wore tuxes. For some reason I wore a blue shirt while everyone else had on white. I stuck out like a sore thumb. My wife and I arrived at the White House gate with our Volkswagen van. We were parked alongside all the Mercedes, Lincolns, Cadillacs, and limousines. At least our vehicle was washed.

All evening I kept calling Henry Kissinger "Pierre Sallinger," which seemed to irritate him. His date was Mamie Van Doren, who I had met before in California. This upset Kissinger, too. For entertainment, the Carpenters were playing and singing, and I became a little confused and kept calling them the Carpetbaggers. This made Henry madder yet. When I mistakenly ate the plant in the finger bowl as a salad, that was all he could take. I never saw him again that night.

HARRY MESHEL

One of my favorite senators was Harry Meshel, the Democrat Minority leader from the other side of the aisle.

We're on the Senate floor one day agreeing and disagreeing the state budget bill. Senator Meshel requests to speak. President Aronoff recognizes the senator from Youngstown. Harry was an eloquent orator, and when he spoke, everyone listened. At the end of his ten-minute dissertation on why he opposed the bill, he finished by saying, ladies and gentlemen, this bill has a certain sweet fragrance that reminds me of the scent of "Equine Petoria." For that reason his vote was no.

Senator Aronoff immediately called for a short intermission. He asked all Republicans to caucus. He asked if any of us knew what Equine Petoria meant. No one knew, so he asked a page to get the answer while we all returned to the Senate floor.

A short time later the page returned waving his hands to Aronoff. The president said, "So what's the answer?" The page said, "Well, Mr. President, the words mean this bill smells like horse s_ _t!"

THE MULE GALLOPS WITH BUTCH CASSIDY
AND THE SUNDANCE KID

My best way to show affection towards someone is to tag them with a nickname. Senators Doug White and Scott Nein became Butch Cassidy and the Sundance Kid.

The more I learned about the reputation of these two cowboys, the more I was certain I named them correctly. As we would leave the State House every night I'd yell, "Hey cowboys, which way in town are you headed tonight? I want to make sure I'm on the other side of town."

Doug White has a caring heart. One day I was quietly grieving the death of my father and writing a eulogy for his funeral service when I felt a firm hand on my shoulder. It was Doug, and he asked if he could sit down. I said, sure. He said, "It's probably none of my business, Coach, but I know you're hurting. Did your father know the Lord?" I said, "Oh, did he ever. He walked with him daily." Doug said, "Well, let's celebrate. We know he's with his maker and wife. Make sure your message is positive." We bonded for life.

Doug's roots are deep in morals, values, and character. He's a low-key persuasive, hard-working kind of guy. His word is his bond. I learned that about him as we worked together trying to solve difficult education and farm issues. Doug is an Ohio State University graduate in the field of animal science. He's a good practical joker. One year as chairman of the agriculture committee, he sent a memo to all new committee members stating they had to perform a Texas sheep castration as part of their initiation to the committee.

I discovered quite quickly Doug's running mate, Scott Nein. Scott is from the southern Ohio town of Middletown. He was born a horse trader. He can sell a dead man toilet paper. He's one of those high-pressure insurance salesmen. When Nein first came to the Senate, he was vice-chairman of the state government committee I chaired. Before committee would begin, I usually told stories about my life on the farm or playing football. As soon as Scott heard a story, he could tell it better than me. Scott and I soon became family.

For some reason, all of us sat close together in the back rows on the Senate floor. We always jumped to each other's defense if we needed support. I don't think there ever was a bill that one of us was carrying that didn't pass.

One time Butch and Sundance invited me to their "Old Fashioned Rodeo" fundraiser. It was held at lobbyist Tom Freis's farm.

I showed up in my blue jeans, T-shirt, cowboy boots, and Stetson hat. I was ready to ride! Give me some horses and bulls and I'll have me some fun! I was stopped at the ring gate. I protested. Security told me I had to show my rodeo-riding license—only professionals could ride. I told them I was born and raised on a farm, and besides, Butch and Sundance personally invited me to partake in all their activities. They finally summoned Doug, who was prancing around the ring on his show horse. He saw I wasn't kidding and calmed me down. Doug not only has his horse- and bull-riding certificate but also a license to race cars. Of course, he likes to rub all that in my face. He truly does live the life of the wild, wild west.

One day Senator White had a meeting with lawyers and the Department of Taxation regarding difference of opinion in taxes. The meeting was being held in the senator's office, and he had to leave before it ended. One of the lawyers said they may need some boxing gloves to continue negotiations after he left. Senator White leaned forward in his chair and said in a quiet, direct voice, "Sir, I was raised in a rough river town, and I'll clue you, we didn't settle differences with boxing gloves." The room became silent. He stood up and said, "Gentlemen, excuse me. My office is yours. I want the issue settled when I return."

SMART KIDS

Being a senator was a real enjoyable and educational experience. I especially liked sharing with students in schools. One time a third-grade student asked me, "Senator, is there anything lower than a senator?"

THE GAME OF POLITICS

A friend of mine once offered some interesting advice early in my political career. He said the major part of the game of football is played between the 20-yard lines. That's where most of the work is done. The outcome is usually decided by the strongest majority.

The same is true in the political arena. Teams from both sides of the legislative aisle spend hours behind closed doors working hard—discussing, debating, compromising on bills before the majority eventually scores. The players then go onstage (the floor united) to play-act how they arrived at their decisions for the media and public to watch. We were a united team, and the citizens were confident we made the right decisions.

Today, the game of politics is played on a larger scale—mainly, from end zone to end zone. Anything goes. Legislators debate and air all their personal agendas on the floor for the whole world to see while trying to justify their feelings. Prior to the recent term limits, the first goal of a legislator was to help the folks back home who elected him or her. Now those people are abandoned to the back row. The priority is more to the deep-pocketed lobbyists to establish contacts for good-paying jobs and appointments after retirement.

DIVINE ENLIGHTENMENT

Throughout my sixteen years serving in Ohio's 19th Senatorial District, I maintained a close relationship with many patriotic ministerial pastors. I'm forever indebted to all of them for their time, encouragement, and trust, especially William Morris, Jerry Durham, and Dan Whisner.

There wasn't a week that went by that one of them didn't pray with me for the wisdom to make good decisions when I voted. Each week there were hundreds of bills—some good, some so-so, some poor.

It's great to know that we are all free people and our greatest freedom is to vote. God has truly blessed America.

CHAPTER TEN

ADVENTURES WITH FAMILY AND FRIENDS

THE BIG DREAM

The year was 1972. I was visiting the small Ohio towns of Loud-onville and Perrysville, located in the middle of Mohican Country. While standing on one hilltop next to a legendary Indian smoke-signal pit, I could see for miles in every direction. I was over-whelmed. My wife and two brothers were with me. We could vi-sualize this area being an outdoor natural Cedar Point, filled with families enjoying recreational activities. My wife named the moun-tain October Hill.

Later that day, I jotted down all the possibilities. We were located close to the Mohican State Park and Forest, and the state-owned Malibar Farm. It could all be tied together with endless activities: hiking, fishing, horseback riding, Snowmobiling, canoeing, kaya-king, tubing, rafting, camping, swimming, archery, horseshoes, putt-putt golf, water slides, Indian pow-wows, Civil War reenact-ments, a triathlon. There could be horse-drawn wagons, buggies, covered wagons, an amphitheater, cabins and camp lots, restau-rants, a dance hall, a small animal pet area, and a grocery store.

In 1973, my wife Judy and I teamed up with my brother Mike to pursue our dream. We secured a bank loan for $1.5 million. Work was 24/7/365. We wanted to concentrate on catering to the out-door crowd. We immediately made three major purchases—a ca-noe livery, rental campgrounds, and a camp lot development. We called it all "October Hill." We tied up another thousand acres with leases and began to build all the amenities mentioned in our vision.

Some of our first lot owners were two great athletes, John Havlicek and Buddy Bell. Performing on weekends at our amphitheater were acts like Ricky Nelson, the Oak Ridge Boys, cast members from TV's *Hee Haw*, and many others. Attending special programs at our Left Tackle Restaurant were Cleveland Browns players Don Cockroft, Brian Sipe, Gregg Pruitt, Doug Dieken, as well as others. As we were in the middle of our construction period (1974–76), a lot of development to the area was also occurring. It made it difficult for tourists to find us. Three of the four roads leading to October Hill were shut off by the following projects: (a) a town streetscape; (b) new downtown bridge; (c) new downtown bypass; (d) new bridge and road to replace Wally Road; (e) expansion of state park area road from two to three lanes.

Besides these projects, interest rates on our loan skyrocketed from 4.5 to 21 percent. During that period, no one could purchase gasoline on weekends because of the national fuel shortage.

Even though we had succeeded in building most of our dream, by the time things returned to normal in 1976, our vision was crushed. It was all over but the shouting. We had to sell or give away everything but the canoe livery. We fought hard to keep it. But with only the one business left, we were like a restaurant that could only cook eggs or a hardware store that could only sell hammers.

Running the livery wasn't all fun and games. Some people got upset if they got wet. Others would sue us if they got scratched by a tree branch. Some were lost on the river past midnight. By 8 a.m. in the morning you had to have everything washed, gassed, and cleaned for the start of a new day.

We were always taking canoes to welders to be fixed. They'd get holes in them and start leaking after scraping over the rocks daily. On an occasional busy day, I'd use duct tape, Band Aids, or even chewing gum to cover a hole. If I was lucky, the canoe would go several hundred yards before the patch popped out. By then the customers figured they came to get wet, so they might as well experience some water sooner as later.

Our business depended on the height of the river. If there wasn't enough water, you couldn't canoe. If the river rose too high, you couldn't canoe. We had a special saying: "Our business is going down the river." There was a lot of truth to that! Even though the business was only in operation four months a year, we had to pay yearly fixed costs. If you never rented out one canoe you still paid the yearly fees. Also, you had to have yearly insurance on buses, vans, and trailers whether you ran them or not. There were daily maintenance costs, and you had to pay people salaries.

Despite all these negatives, the canoe livery was a great working family business. It gave us a way to be together in the summer. Everybody worked as a team. My kids will tell you I treated them like slaves, but my wife and I worked hard, too. It was like being back on the farm working with my dad.

Gerrit and Isaac, the youngest of my seven children, were the entertainment when they were age six and four. They'd ride their tricycles into the water for laughs or turn a water hose on people and squirt them. When each of my five boys and two daughters reached about age twelve, I taught them to drive vans, trucks, and buses. They'd practice driving by the hours in our parking lot and on the quiet road across from our business. They learned to back up single and double trailers by age thirteen. They started driving the vans and picking up canoes as early as age fifteen. At sixteen they could safely ferry people back to their starting point. They were all responsible and excellent drivers. Passengers would sometimes ask them, "Do you have a driver's license?" They'd politely say, "Yes ma'am" or "Yes, sir." Sometimes a cop would be parked along the road while they were driving. They'd usually stretch up a little higher in the seat and give him a friendly wave.

Later, we had to have licensed CDL drivers to drive passengers on all buses and some vans. These drivers were hard to find in our small area.

One time I was driving a busload of about fifty canoers back to their cars in Loudonville. It was a fifteen-mile trip and I was following my fifteen-year-old son Jeff, who was driving a truck pulling two trailers loaded with sixteen canoes.

As Jeff came to a sharp bend in the road, I could see he was in trouble. There was a fast-approaching empty bus coming at him. I held my breath and prayed, expecting the worst. Jeff went straight ahead into a hayfield, bouncing up and down like crazy holding on to the wheel, but thank God he came to a safe stop. Everyone in the bus was talking about the kid bouncing through the field, and boy, were they laughing and razzing him.

I acted like I didn't know him very well. He looked okay. As soon as my passengers all unloaded in Loudonville, I talked to him. He was still pretty shaken but glad I had stopped for him. He thought I was going to be mad. I wrestled him to the ground and then apologized and said how proud I was and how happy I was that he was safe. Jeff was always a good, safe driver. He got even with me for playing around with him a short time later—tackled me from behind and knocked me in the river. I chased him for twenty minutes but couldn't catch him. Never did get even. Someday I will.

When we were really busy, Gerrit and Isaac had to help launch canoes. Some people didn't have very good balance or they were overweight and would fall into the water, taking the boys with them. Then they both had to help the people get their canoe right side up and start them off down the river again.

It was even more amusing at the finish. Some of the canoeists would have a few drinks and couldn't stand up very well. Some might be sitting in the bottom of the canoe or hanging on to their canoe in the middle of the river. We'd help them to stand up and get to dry land. The river was only one- to three-feet deep. If anyone fell in, we'd yell to them, "Just stand up! It's only knee deep!"

BEAR FLIRTS WITH MULE

From 1973 to 1986, I attended all the Ohio sports and recreation shows, promoting the Mohican area and our recreation business. Almost everywhere I went, a wrestling bear was there, too. His name was Victor. His owner kept him muzzled, and he was declawed, as well. He had been trained to wrestle people since he was a baby cub. Victor weighed about six hundred pounds and stood close to ten feet tall. I never saw him hurt anyone seriously. For a dollar you could wrestle him. My brother Mike and I would occasionally take a whack at him. He would play with me at times, rolling around together. Then, when he was ready, he'd flatten me to the canvas. A few times he knocked the air out of me or, better yet, popped my spine like a chiropractor. It got so that he started looking for me. His owner and promoters paid me to wrestle him.

We had fun rolling around in the ring together. I actually think he liked being around me. Maybe it was the mule smell? Maybe it was true love? Victor's owner even brought him to my canoe livery a few times during the summer months. He said Victor got lonesome for me. He loved to chug Cokes and eat Tootsie Rolls! I could even get him into a canoe with me for a short ride, but then the canoe would sink to the bottom because of our weight.

Victor goes and gets sick and dies right before opening night at a Cleveland show in 1978. A friend of mine, Joe Madigan, called me and said, "Schaf, I have a great deal for you. Your friend Victor died, but we'd like to have you pose as him for the weekend and wrestle people." He offered me free booth space at the Convention Center to promote my canoe livery and gave me $100 per forty-five minute session—three times a day—to wrestle people while posing as Victor. It sounded okay with me.

Joe sent me to a local costume shop to be fitted to look like a bear. Then I stopped to see a former All-American wrestling champion and Hall of Famer Gene Weiss. Gene's been a close friend since the 1950s at Ohio State. He spent fifteen to twenty minutes teaching me a couple of basic moves, gave me his own wrestling mat to use, and said, "You're ready, Victor Schaf. Go get 'em!"

I also involved two of my sons. Three-year-old Gerrit was dressed in a tux, including tall top hat, whip, and a lead chain. He was to lead me on and off the stage with a rope. My other son, Ty, sixteen, was the referee. He had a referee's whistle tied around his neck. My orders to him were to count my opponents out and blow the whistle as soon as they touched the canvas. After a few growls, I was ready to tackle everybody!

Things started out pretty good, but after jumping and racing around the stage tussling with a couple dozen contestants, I started to wear out fast. I couldn't breathe in the hot suit with the bear head on. I was sweating like crazy and became completely dehydrated. I rolled off the back of the stage, begging for water and for Ty to take my bear head off. He couldn't. It was sewn on tight.

Ty quickly unrolled a nearby four-inch cloth fire hose, which was wrapped around a steel post. He opened my nose mask enough to stick the hose down the neck of my suit. We both worked at pushing the hose down until it reached my stomach area. As I lay gasping for air on the cement floor, he turned the water on full blast! The water came out with such force that it blew me wiggling out past the stage area, where I hit a few people and knocked down some chairs. I went sliding and wiggling on my back about a hundred feet into the audience. I was flat on my back, and water was squirting out of holes in my suit from head to toe.

Parents were in shock, and kids were screaming and crying. The bear is leaking; the bear is dying! Boy, that water felt good! Later they took me to a local hospital. I was dehydrated. They fed me liquids intravenously for a couple of hours and I was fine. That was the last time Victor wrestled. He was officially pronounced dead.

MULE AGAINST MULE

At our recreational facility we sold camp lots. At the entrance area we let a miniature mule run loose all day. His name was Corn Cobb. He loved to play tug-of-war with me. I kept the rope in my back pocket when I was busy welcoming people. When Cobb wanted to play he'd approach me from behind and take the rope from my pocket. I always had to drop everything I was doing for a short time and challenge him. Customers always got a kick out of our little game. Whoever won got to eat an ear of corn. I always made sure Corn Cobb did.

BUSINESS AS USUAL

My daughter Heidi ran the canoe business from age ten on. She answered phones, handled workers, signed up canoers, explained length of trips, and handled the money most of the time by herself.

She worked from 8 a.m. until the last canoe was in, sometimes as late as 8 or 9 p.m. We all called her "Mouse."

To show her cleverness, one time while she was busy she received a phone call for some canoe information. She waved to brother Bruin, age eight, to come to the phone when the customer asked if anyone older could take her call. She whispered to Bruin to sound old. He tried to use a deep voice, but that didn't work. They finally found me. The customer was in stitches laughing.

I had Ty and two other boys working at our first canoe-livery landing where nine-mile canoers ended the trip. Ty was always my old reliable. It was toward the end of the day, and I took the two other boys home. I forgot I had sent out a group of fifty canoes, which hadn't arrived back yet. An hour later, I was driving down the road looking for stragglers. All of a sudden I see Ty out in the middle of the road waving his arms at me to stop. I said, "What are you doing out here in the road?" He said, "Dad, there's canoers coming in from everywhere. I don't know what to do." I said, race your butt back to the landing and help them. You can't be any good standing up here on the road. I drove in to help him. It was chaos for a half hour or so, but we finally got everything under control. I then apologized for my mistake, and we both laughed at his behavior. He didn't think it was as funny as I did. Ty was always my clean-up hitter, making sure everything was in the barn before we locked up for the night.

SURPRISE REVIVAL AT THE RIVER

One day I picked up a busload of passengers who had been canoeing all day. Thirty-five of them were from a Baptist church, but the other sixteen had been out smoking pot and drinking beer. Sensing possible trouble, I asked them if it would be okay to all ride together. It was a twenty-minute trip back to their cars. They all said no problem. I thought, Lord, help us this ride; this is going to be something. Half were singing rock; half were singing gospel.

I was traveling slowly along a dirt road that followed the river. The road was soft from a lot of rain earlier in the week. Everything was going fine when a passing car comes at me. I stopped as far to side of the road as I could get. We sat there for two or three seconds, when all of a sudden the side of the bank started giving way. The bus was quickly on its side sliding to the bottom of the bank adjacent to the river. I was hanging on to the wheel, feet on ceiling, until the bus was nearly upside down and came to crashing stop. I could hear windows breaking as we clipped off some small trees on way down.

I was sure many were hurt, if not dead, and quickly started to try to help. People were sideways, upside down, and crawling over each other. Somehow, somebody had opened the back door, and everyone was helping everyone else. After checking the inside a couple times, I was the last one out. I quickly surveyed the situation and it was unbelievable—a miracle was happening. No one was seriously hurt—just cuts and bruises. Everyone was hugging each other and praising the Lord. Even the nonbelievers.

One of the people happened to be a minister. He said anyone wishing to could kneel with him and give a prayer of thanks. A few people started to grasp hands. Pretty soon we all were holding hands, kneeling, and praying by the river—the churchgoers and smokers and drinkers.

A fire truck, some ambulances, and another bus arrived a short time later and took us back to the parking lot. Everyone was thanking me for the great experience. One hippie said, "I wanted to change my life for a long time. I guess this is as good a time as any to start." Not one person sued me or the canoe business.

BUSINESS IS TOUGH

In addition to my family, we needed ten workers, but some of the time we only had five. You had to have workers that would show up. You didn't know when to put them on the clock or send them home because of the height of the river. The water was always up and down, up and down. A third of the time the water was too high, making it unsafe to canoe. We'd have to shut the place down on busy days and give money back.

It's tough to run any private business today.

From the 1970s through the 1990s too many government regulations and mandates were added to burden small businesses. A constant stream of more regulations, restrictions, mandates, subsidies, union rules, health-care costs, insurance costs, tax abatements, entitlements, OSHA regulations, and soaring gas and utility costs. We had to pay attention to minimum wage, prevailing wage, affirmative action, workers' age requirements, and worker's comp. All this in addition to our normal accounting, phones, advertising and downtime lost, plus tons of needless paperwork. Get behind on your loans to the bank or taxes to the government and pay for it with massive penalties. You're forced to quit or borrow more money to make these additional payments.

And then came the layers of taxes: Income, personal, corporate, sales, equipment, fuel, property inheritance, franchise, and more. Ohio is one of the worst states (third) to own and operate a business. We've succeeded in driving most small family-owned businesses out of our state. Yet over the past forty years, the state's operating budget has grown from $1.5 billion to $50.5 billion. Big government keeps getting bigger and bigger.

I sold the canoe livery in 1997. After twenty-five years, I broke even. I paid myself to have a job, but it was fun. I wouldn't have traded those days for any amount of money. I met thousands of great people, and my kids learned how to be responsible, work hard, and run a business.

A FAMILY TRIP AROUND THE U.S.

In 1982, our family took a three-month trip around the United States and Canada. Twenty-five thousand miles, thirty-two states, five kids, Judy, and me. The kids were ages 3, 5, 8, 10, and 15, all old enough to know better. We traveled in an extra-length Dodge Star Craft van. Our budget was $7 per person per meal. We took our school-age kids out of school with the official's permission and started the trip in mid-November.

It started to get cold and snowy as we headed west. Our trail was designed to cover mostly back roads. Rugged, dirty, seldom covered back roads. At times, all seven of us became mortal enemies.

Unless someone bled, there were no rules in the van. We wore sweat suits for travel and sleep. We each had pockets in the sweats to carry our own soap, toothbrush, and toothpaste. When we left the van for the restroom, we pretended we did not know each other. We were only allowed to grunt, nod, or give hand signals. We didn't want anyone to know that we were a family traveling together, afraid that business owners would report us for using their facilities for free. Yeah, right. Like our sweat suits didn't give our identity away? We slept in the van every night in sleeping bags at great places like truck stops, car dealerships, rest stops, hotel parking lots, gas stations, restaurants, and so forth. We were not particular. (Though after a while the girls started to rebel because of having to go to the bathroom occasionally along the side of the road like the boys. At one of these frequent pit stops somewhere in Iowa, they locked me out of the van and made me walk until I promised, in writing, that they could go to the bathroom in lighted rest stop areas.)

Sleeping in the van was tricky and comical at times, and each child had a task to make the routine work, like closing curtains so people could not see in, getting the sleeping bags ready, and rolling down seats for beds. Most nights were freezing in the van, and we all wore wool hats. My mom told me before we left, "No way seven people can make that trip. I bet you don't make it a week."

Isaac, age two, was a bit of a problem. He was always stepping in slush or mud puddles then getting everything dirty in the van, pooping his pants, or yelling, "I'm hungry" or "I'm thirsty." The other kids made a game of grading his smelly diapers on a scale of one to five. Usually it was always a five-plus! We were parked by a snow bank at a potty stop in Vancouver, Canada, when he said, Daddy I'm thirsty! I told him to stick his head in that snow bank there and suck. Everybody got a kick out of that, except his mom. I can't remember if he did it or not.

About a week into the trip, we were getting on each other's nerves. The girls rebelled one night and locked me out of the van, refusing to let me in until I promised to make frequent stops at lighted, indoor restrooms; they were sick of going in the bushes with the boys. When I next called my mom, she asked me how it was going. I told her I now knew how Noah must have felt on the ark.

We opted to take mostly rural, scenic roads, rarely driving on highways. Many of these roads afforded beautiful views but seldom had guardrails. My fear of heights became a problem when climbing those single-lane mountain cliff roads or even crossing high bridges. Judy or Ty was then forced to drive.

Each place we visited was a story on its own. The three oldest kids kept daily diaries. Heidi lost hers in Texas in a garbage dumpster. After driving across the edge of two states, we discovered her loss and had to go back. We drove all night. Yep, it was still there! The kids did their school assignments. We saw President Reagan at the White House in Washington. (Of course, Isaac had a black eye; he fell down some steps the night before while sleepwalking.) We saw several Indian reservations. We visited Little Big Horn, where Custer was killed. We saw Mount Rushmore and a big statue of Paul Bunyon and his ox, Babe. Traveled to the head of the Mississippi River in Minnesota and saw the other end in New Orleans. We visited the Dakota Badlands. Saw cattle drives in Wyoming and walked some of the Grand Canyon in Arizona. Saw potato farms in Idaho, the Redwood Forest in California, the Rockies, and Mt. Saint Helens in Washington. Moose, bear, sheep, coyote, donkey, and buffalo approached our van when we stopped. We swam in the hot mineral springs in the snowy western mountains.

Visited Yosemite National Park, the Hearst Castle, the San Diego Zoo, the Rose Bowl, Disneyland, and several movie-star homes in Beverly Hills. We even slept next to one in our van. I got out to go to the bathroom in the middle of the night, and when I returned to the van, I realized there was something stuck to my shoe. I couldn't see, so I ran my finger across my shoe. The worse possible scenario—I'd stepped in dog doo. Boy, did that smell. I wiped my finger off the best I could and then rolled the window down enough to be able to sleep with my shoe and finger outside the van.

We went to the car wash early the next morning so I could wash my hands and clean the floor and my shoe! We visited old covered wagon trails, Yellowstone, and Old Faithful. We crossed the border into Mexico for a day, where I bought a wooden chicken with no butt. Visited "Old Tucson," where a lot of cowboy movies were filmed. Saw the Alamo in Texas, Thomas Jefferson's Monticello in Virginia, George Washington's home in Mount Vernon, the New York skyscrapers, Boston, the sand dunes at Cape Cod, Cape Canaveral, Florida, cotton fields in Louisiana, and the Carolina beaches. While visiting Vancouver, we met and talked with a woman whose father died on the *Titanic*.

Afterwards, we all had an appreciation for the basics, especially clean clothes, beds, and showers. The kids learned to play a lot of car games like counting cars, telephone poles, cows, and horses. We sang songs and told stories by the hours. We lived a lifetime adventure together that few families ever have a chance at doing.

CANOEING ACROSS LAKE ERIE

Erie-Aue, Canada to Cleveland Flats, 79 miles, 17½ hours, nonstop paddling in a 17-foot aluminum canoe.

As far as I know, no one has ever attempted to canoe across that big puddle. We inquired with the Guinness Book of World Records, and they hadn't either. This challenge constantly intrigued me since I'm scared to death of water. I do not know how to swim and, unfortunately, I get seasick.

The first time I tried canoeing across the lake was with a former disc jockey from Cleveland. I was serious. He did it for publicity. Once we started paddling, he was not prepared to go more than a couple miles. As luck would have it, the waves were awful, most being six feet high, constantly crashing into us. I was so seasick before reaching three miles that I called the disastrous trip off before he did. The next time I vowed to be better prepared. My target for a partner was another radio/TV man, good friend Casey Coleman.

Casey is the well-known son of Ken Coleman, both outstanding Cleveland radio sports personalities. When Casey was a young-

ster back in the 1960s, his dad brought him to the Browns training camp at Hiram College and we quickly became friends. I sold
Casey on the idea of canoeing Lake Erie by pointing out that Native Americans surely must have done it before, so why not us? He
agreed with my logic and was as confident and serious as me.

The weather, however, would just not cooperate. Rough seas
delayed our starting six or seven hours until we decided to go for
it anyway, but the battering waves made it nearly impossible to
canoe. Vince Cellini, a local sports reporter, was trying to report
our feat from a lead boat, but after a mile his face was greener than
mine. He now works for CNN, and my family still refers to him as
Vince the green prince. Sadly, we were towed back to shore like
scolded puppies.

It took a couple years before I thought about trying again. I also
had another battle to contend with, having found out I had stomach and intestinal cancer. While undergoing successful surgery at
the Cleveland Clinic, I had a wonderful roommate, Sam Cain, who
had cancer, too. Sam and I became close friends. We shared our
dreams, families, and our faith in God. After Sam's surgery, he was
told he had three months to live. He and I stayed in touch until he
passed in 1988.

Many people quit because of a setback or problem, but I'm
convinced that with determination, everyone who tackles a challenge can enjoy success. I was passionate about crossing the lake.
I asked for donations in Sam's name to help with cancer research.
We raised over $2,000 and put together a committed team that in-
cluded local weatherman Dick Goddard and the U.S. Coast Guard
weather experts. Together we agreed that mid-August would be the
best chance for mild weather. Also, it would be best to try to start
from Canada. We picked a day, and it was a go.

Jim McIntire was captain of the boat we were to follow. My good
friend Lenny Weiss and my daughter Heidi went along for the ride.
For this trip, I picked Francis "Wolfman" Steel to partner with.
Wolf was quiet, wiry, and tough. He had worked for me at our ca-
noe livery for ten years. My brother Mike was with our friend Brent
Durham in a second canoe. Captain Jim towed our canoes eighty

miles across the lake. On the way, I told Wolfman he was the only man who could steer the canoe. My job was to pull us across. He said, Okay, boss, let's do it.

I was thinking of my friend Sam Cain when at 9 p.m., as the sun was setting, we shoved off into the fairly calm and warm waters of Lake Erie. About five miles into the trip, the weather was still good. I knew I'd make it if I didn't give up physically, and I was not about to do that.

After a few hours pulling hard, I began hurting as bad as I had running the sixty-two miles to Wooster. I tried not to think about it. At one point, Wolfman and I got lost from the lead boat for over an hour in total darkness, but with a lot of yelling we reconnected. One for the book is how to canoe and go to the bathroom. We paddled through two thunderstorms and encountered several big ocean liners in the middle of the lake. At the time, their lights seemed to be an amphitheater in Cleveland. Mike and Brent's canoe sank sometime during the night, but they were safe on Jim's boat.

I'll never forget Lenny in the lead boat, always sitting in his chair with his feet up, sunglasses on, and drinking a beer—the picture of relaxation. Occasionally, he'd yell to me, "Come on, Schaf, I know you can do it," with a broad smile on his face. I wanted to kill him. After the plight was over, I met his mother and she said to me, "Oh, so you're the guy that made my Lenny take that dangerous trip across the lake. I was worried to death about him the whole time. Thank God he's all right."

Wolfman was a great choice! We arrived in the Cleveland Flats t 2:30 in the afternoon. The last five miles paddling to Cleveland was incredible—news helicopters hovered overhead and countless boats surrounded us, honking their approval and yelling encouragements as we paddled to the Flats and shore. When we finally made it to the dock, Wolfman and I were pulled from the canoe and laid to rest in the grass. After a few interviews, still flat on my back, it was decided I'd better be taken to the hospital, so off I went, even though I forcefully tried to refuse.

I rested at the hospital for a couple hours before abruptly checking myself out amidst the doctors and nurses having fits. We walked about a mile back to the Yacht Club where I had parked my car the night before, and Heidi, Mike, and I drove the lone canoe back home. Someone recently asked me if I would ever try that trip again. I quickly replied, No way, you've got to be crazy to canoe that lake! In retrospect, the Lord shined on me with that stunt. I like to think Sam helped.

CHAPTER ELEVEN

THE HEART OF THIS MULE

BACK TO SCHOOL

I was a college student for 51 years.

During that time I was a whole lot of other things—a professional football player, a ranch hand, a bear wrestler, a small business owner, and a state senator in the Ohio General Assembly. But I never was a college graduate. During my first stint as a student, I was able to have a lot of success as an athlete. But I never closed the deal and got my degree, despite what I had promised my mom and Woody Hayes.

In the fall of 2004, I asked Ohio State University to allow me to return to school full time with the intention of finishing my degree. I immediately encountered a six-month delay while people in the university administration searched the "vault" looking for clues to my past academic heroics. After considerable detective work, they located my records and dusted them off. It was determined that I still needed a minimum of 46 credit hours to receive my undergraduate degree. Moreover, at the time I ended my first run at college, my GPA was a whopping 1.9999. I guess you could say I had room for some improvement.

In the spring of 2005, after about fifty years, I was back on campus again. To say the world of being a college student has changed since the mid-1950s would be an understatement.

My first two courses were history. I was intimidated and a nervous wreck for the first few weeks. I could barely remember my name. I spoke to my professor after class, who told me to relax and enjoy the experience, that I had a lot to offer—especially since I had lived through most of the time period we were studying! I wasn't sure if he was kidding or serious.

I loved the learning experience, but at my age, it was the re-membering part that presented the most challenges. I quickly re-connected with the library for assistance. Not only had the school library grown tenfold, but there were now these things called com-puters and a place called the Internet. Oh boy, was I in a strange land. Here I was on a campus with 50,000 students, and I was prob-ably the only one who didn't use *any* of this modern technology. I must have looked like quite the sight with my old Roy Rogers/Dale Evans metal lunch box for the 1940s and carrying my books in an empty cat litter bucket. But thanks to everyone's help and patience, I learned to navigate in this new world.

At the age of sixty-nine, I carried a whistle around my neck for protection. There were a lot of beautiful girls all over campus, and you can never tell when one of them might try to attack. At my age, I might have trouble fighting them off. It never happened, but I didn't want to take any chances.

Shortly after starting school, I stopped by head coach Jim Tres-sel's office for a chat. I reminded him that since I was not allowed to play football as a freshmen way back when, I believed I still had a year of eligibility left. "What do you think, Coach?" With-out skipping a beat, Coach said, "Yeah, Mule, we'll call you our se-cret weapon, but let's just keep it our secret and forget about the weapon part!"

When I re-entered school, some media asked to interview me about my new education experience. I declined until I was done with all my class work, though. I was scared. I didn't want to talk about how great it was to be back in school, accomplishing one of my life goals, then fall on my face by flunking a course.

I kept constant pressure on myself to do well. I was extremely fortunate that in the second half of my college life, I never received a grade lower than a "B." I keep thinking I should have a T-shirt made that reads. "1.9999 and still rising!"

My family and friends called periodically to see how I was doing, but it is fair to say that I was all consumed by my re-entry into the world of higher education.

In early 1950s, I had a high school coach who was a good motivator. Two of his best slogans were: "You gotta wanna," and "There are no guarantees." He was right on. Life to me is all about overcoming challenges and pursuing different opportunities. And as long as I'm still alive, I intend to climb more mountains.

At my age, I still believe you can accomplish most anything if you want it bad enough. Like everyone, I have a few aches and pains—the arthritis family has invaded most of my joints. I have poor vision and have to have all my reading and notes enlarged. My hands shake when I get nervous, and I have difficulty writing. I have had two cancer operations. I have a pacemaker fibulator wired to my heart. I bleed easily and have died fifty times over the past five years. Other than those few setbacks, I'm ready to continue to play the game of life. If I can do it, anyone can. If you don't have an opportunity—make one!

I have learned how important it is that we not take our opportunities lightly. A whole lot of people sacrificed a whole lot for me to have accomplished some exciting goals. My parents encouraged and supported most everything I've tried. They were always hopeful that I would one day go back to school and complete my degree. While I was a state senator, some peers suggested I apply for an honorary degree to satisfy my parents' wishes. I declined, saying they did not like fake things. If I didn't earn it, they would not appreciate it. (However, I did tell my daughter Heidi while I was back in school that if I died before obtaining my degree, she should find a diploma—fake or not—and throw it into my casket. I wouldn't want to see my parents without it!)

MY FAMILY

I was married to my first wife, Bonnie, from 1957–67. Together we had three children: Jeff, Renée, and Ty. From 1968–84, I was married to my second wife, Judy. We had four children together: Heidi, Bruin, Gerrit, and Isaac.

I wasn't the perfect husband or father. I took vows for better or

worse, but when trouble arose, I turned and ran. I'm not proud of
my failed marriages and have always tried to be open and honest
with my kids abut it.

Divorce is not a good thing, especially for children. It carries a
bushel of hurts. I always loved my kids and wanted to be the best
dad I could. But just wanting wasn't enough. Being a good parent is
the hardest thing in the world to do. There are so many emotions,
so much you have to learn the hard way, so many unintentional
mistakes. Even for married fathers, it is a challenge to be present
and accounted for in a child's daily upbringing. It was all the more
difficult being a divorced dad and having ex-wives living in Chicago
and Connecticut.

But it's hardest on the kids. I have thought many times how in-
credibly difficult it must have been for my children to whether to
live with their mother or with me. Two of my children chose me.
Five did not. This had to be a very emotional decision—a lasting
scar for all of them. I know it was hard for me, and I was a grown
adult. It was always so sad saying good-byes.

After each of my divorces, I knew it was up to me to maintain
a connection. I kept in touch with my children as much as I could
throughout each year and looked forward to the two weeks we
were united during the summer. For much of their formative years
I owned a canoe livery. I thought that would be a great place to
teach them what I learned from my dad: the value of an honest
day's work. It also gave me the opportunity to share my love for the
outdoors and animals. As I look back, though, I suppose I pushed
them harder than I should have. Still, each summer we all came
together and created new memories and stories—many of which
we look back on today and laugh about until we have tears stream-
ing down our faces. Despite our limited time, we've experienced a
lot together.

MY CHILDREN

Of all the many life experiences I've had, none comes close to
the joy of being the father of my seven beautiful kids. I am truly

blessed having had their presence in my life. I am grateful I've lived long enough to see them make their own way through this changing world, each one experiencing a journey of ups and downs, but ultimately, of rewards and meaning.

Jeff is great musician, he can play all instruments, and he's an excellent singer. He's tall, strong, good-looking. Jeff lived with his mom through high school in the Chicago area. He tried to live with me in Ohio to play football, but at the same time I started coaching for the Washington Redskins. Jeff was a super baby. He walked at ten months, said his ABCs and, counted to one hundred before his first birthday. Jeff and his wife, Sue, have two children, Garrison and Cambria. They live in California.

Renée was my first princess. She was born with club feet but grew out of the problem after wearing correction casts for two years. She lived with her mom through high school but loved visiting Grandmaw's farm in Ohio. She was always talking to, feeding, or petting horses, cows, chickens, and cats. She raised four sons who became Eagle Scouts. She loves to act and entertain, and she works at DisneyWorld wearing different animated cartoon character costumes all day. She is very independent. Renée and her husband, John, have five children, Nathan, Andrew, Ryan, Evon, and Justin. They live in Florida.

Ty lives Florida. He lived with me through high school. He had two nicknames: "Hoss" (after TV character Hoss Cartright) and "Baloney" (he, like me, is a big eater). A good athlete, he played all sports in high school and football at Ohio Wesleyan. He graduated from The Ohio State University. He loves to try and challenge me in one-on-one sports. He's also smart and artistic. (He worked for Nickelodeon on the drawing board of *SpongeBob SquarePants* and *The Angry Beavers*).

Heidi, my second princess, lived with me through high school. She's extremely talented, responsible, faithful, and dependable. She's street- smart, too. She loves to read and is an authority on history. Heidi operated and managed our canoe livery at age twelve, then helped me campaign throughout my career as senator. At fourteen she drove me to many meetings and speaking engagements. She missed her mom and brothers a lot. We both shed big tears. She and her husband, David, live in Ohio and own a construction business.

Bruin is one smart, tough kid. I tried to name him "Bo Savage." Has a lot of endurance, and, like me, he can get a little rowdy. He lived with mother through most of his school years. He should be a racecar driver or big-game hunter—he has no fear. And he's an excellent carpenter by trade. He and his wife, Melissa, have two children, Cole and Rune. They live in Connecticut.

Gerrit lived with mother all through his school years. He tried to live with me once but didn't like that I was seldom home. Extremely well-rounded, Gerrit has a lot of common sense. He played all sports in high school, and lacrosse at Johns Hopkins. He's a graduate of The Ohio State University and works for the Goldman Sachs investment firm. He and his wife, Svitlana have one child, Misha. They live in Massachussets.

Isaac always lived with his mother. He, too, played all sports in high school, and he played lacrosse at Butler University. Has a lot of natural talent and the potential to be successful at anything he tries. He now lives in Connecticut and works with a watch-making company. I know we both miss knowing each other better. He has one child, Xaven, who lives with his mother, Ashley.

With a mule mentality, I was a pretty slow learner. I made a lot of bad choices, but despite them my kids still turned out as fine people. I'm trying to gain back some of the territory I've lost with them over the years. Like the words in the old song say, "I've gotta keep on truckin' because I've got a long way to go, and a short time to get there."

MY PERSONAL TESTIMONY

I have to admit there are many similarities between me and my mule friends. Looks—except for ears and tail. Smell—they have a slight edge. Teeth and toenails—they win. I also lose on hair and heart size. They probably can outwit, outrun, outeat, and outdrink me. They're louder and put more in the toilet. I can be more stubborn and ornery. But the one thing that sets us apart is my salvation and God's gift of my eternal adventurous heart. When my earthly life ends, my spirit will continue in paradise with the Lord forever.

About ten years ago I fell dead in a parking lot. I was quickly revived by Nick Williams, Bill Adams, and my doctor, Dr. Polinsky. Doc says that normally people in my condition have three to five years to live. But I like my friend Joe Frazier's take on this better: "I know I will stop breathing when God rings the bell. Not a second sooner." I do have a safety battery wired into my heart to bang me if it stops. Recently, Doc was checking my ticker for its recording over the past six months. He said, "Mule, as I'm reading your chart it says your device fired eight times, and it was in the red zone ready to fire fifty-five times. I keep telling you your pumper is about finished. Whatever you're doing, change it. There is no reserve left. There are no more opportunities for hustle and second effort. You're close to the list for a heart transplant."

BINGO! The elevator finally went to the top floor. His words hit me like a royal flush. No matter how hard I try, my body will be finished sometime in near future. There's no security, immunity, or guarantee that anyone can purchase for living on this earth forever. But we can have an eternal spiritual heart. It's free for the asking.

Everything we do takes courage. President Kennedy said, "The stories of courage can define the point one wants to reach, but they can't supply the courage itself. For this a person has to look into his own heart." Does your heart shine with light, or is it moving in the darkness?

I've had a lot of fun and great times chasing dreams. But in the end, obtaining worldly dreams is not sustaining. They quickly become old memories. Kinda like a bunch of us old codgers sitting around the room talking about the good old days.

By the way, God and I are working on my latest challenge: to be the oldest Ohioan ever to have lived. The stumbling block between us is still how much God will slow down my aging process. Only time will tell.

IN THE END IS THE BEGINNING

The older I get, the more frequently I look back on my early years on the family farm. I think of those beautiful, soft rolling hills in Wayne County. They always looked so quiet, yet they were always so demanding of time and energy. Those winding dirt roads were dusty and bumpy, and isn't life that way?

I love recalling the four seasons of the year as the Native Americans use to refer to them.

Spring (Planting Moon): The land would burst into green. The freshly plowed fields looked so fresh. Work and joy seemed to pull together. I often thought that same thing going to football camp—full of anticipation and hope for the coming season.

Summer (Corn Harvest Moon): The fields were alive with crops and those magnificent sunsets. It was exciting to see groups of men and Mother Nature working together. Only God could create such an awesome event.

Fall (Falling Leaves Moon): It was special on the farm. Harvest time. It was time to reap the reward of our efforts. Seeing the cornstalks all standing tall in row after row across the fields was like a sign reading "job well done." And pumpkins and tree foliage all expressed their approval with so much color.

Winter (Maple Moon): Could be harsh, but the snow was an exciting, breathtaking picture. The biting cold was a reminder that beauty can be brutal, but spring wasn't far away.

Yes, life on the farm was a road map of the rest of my life.

ACKNOWLEDGMENTS

I'd like to thank Mom and Dad for living by the Ten Commandments and for their unwavering love and respect for family.

I'd like to give a special thanks to my typist. No other person or persons are qualified to understand me or translate my language like Pastor Jean and her "mule" husband, Pastor Jack. Without them I was like a chicken pecking for corn. Our daily slogan—"Lord, we're starting to get it now."

Good friend Chuck Such for much-needed advice and helpful information. Brother Larry, who gave me much-needed suggestions, Gary Parks for his continuous help and encouragement, and, finally, George Buksar for help with football history research.

For their support during my second stint at The Ohio State University, I am especially grateful to my Youngstown Connection: Coach Jim Tressel, Bruce Zoldan, and Jim Ward. All three are very special men, and I am deeply appreciative of their continuous support. Also, thanks to my classmates and instructors, The Ohio State University Office of Student Athletics, and the Office of Disability Services.

Many people have knowingly and unknowingly contributed to the content of this book. Some have agreed to be recognized while others prefer anonymity. Some will be surprised and/or disappointed to find their name in print, but to all, the intent of documenting my life story has never been to offend any person, place, organization, political party, or animal. I also should note that after thirteen NFL seasons and three marriages, I've probably forgotten more than I remember. If I've excluded anyone, I sincerely apologize.

Special thanks to Mel Adelman, George Allen, Stan Aronoff, Doug Atkins, Nick Baird, Roy Bates, Tim Barrett, Jess Bell, Rick Bell, Ken Blair, Kathleen Blubaugh, Jim Bollman, John Bozick, Jim Brown, Mike Brown, Paul Brown, George Buksar, Dean Chance, Warren Chavers, Monte Clark, Gene Coleman, Blanton Collier, Kay Collier, Gary Collins, Joe Costa, Don Crow, Jimmy Crum, Jeep Davis, Albert Dubenion, Pastor Jerry Durham, fellow Ohio legislators, Kirk Ferentz, former coaches, former teachers, former teammates, Governor Richard Celeste, Bob Gain, Larry Golden,

Jackie Goodway, Bill Granholm, Ernie Green, Dick Gregory, Tim Gren-
dell, Judy Grimm, Jack Hannah, Bill Harris, Anne Hayes, Woody Hayes,
Evelyn Heisler, Fritz Heisler, Kitty Helber and Festus the Mule, Gene
Hickerson, Joe Horrigan, Debby Bramlage-Huters, Carol Kaulfman, Mike
Kiggin, Tom Kiser, Bob Knight, Diana Kohuri, Morrie Kono, Bonnie Ku-
bin, George Lamb, Pat Leahy, Dick LeBeau, Hal Lebovitz, Hal Lechler,
Lee Leonard, Bill Long, Dino Lucarelli, Sam Lucarelli, Mike Lucci, Jim
Mauro, Paula Mauro, Lt. John Mays, Pete McCauley, Bob McEaneney,
Stephanie McEaneney, Darrin Meeker, Jim Mermis, Ken Miller, Bobby
Mitchell, Art Modell, Mom and Dad, Rose Monte, Cy Morgan, Sam Mor-
gan, Pastor William Morris, Bill Myles, Brian Neal, Leslie Neilson, Scott
Nine, OSU-Animal Science, Patricia Owens, Tom Pappas, Geri Pastor, Ber-
nie Parrish, Renée Powell, President Richard M. Nixon, President Ronald
Reagan, Billy Reynolds, Professional Football Hall of Fame staff, Andy
Robustelli, Jan Rus, Bernard Schafrath, Ed Schafrath, Larry Schafrath,
Mike Schafrath, Bo Schembechler, Jim Schmidtke, Larry Siegfried, Char-
ley Smail, soldiers who fought in Vietnam, Frances Steele, Paul Tiber, Paul
Tipps, Eddie Ulinski, Victor the Bear, Julie Ward, Nicholas Ward, Ruthel-
len Weaver, Gene Weiss, Don Welsh, Bill Wentz, Aaron Wheeler, Doug
White, Pastor Dan, and my seven children, especially Renée Raper, Heidi
Hoffmann, and Ty Schafrath.